SYMPOSIUM ON LOVE

Edited by
MARY ELLEN CURTIN

Clinical Research Psychologist
Veterans Administration Hospital
Lexington, Kentucky

BEHAVIORAL PUBLICATIONS
New York
1973

Library of Congress Catalog Number 73-10475

ISBN 0-87705-116-X

BEHAVIORAL PUBLICATIONS
72 Fifth Avenue
New York, New York 10011
Printed in the United States of America

This printing 10 9 8 7 6 5 4 3 2 1

Library of Congress Cataloging in Publication Data
Main entry under title:

Symposium on love. .

    Eight of the 14 papers were presented at 2 meetings of the American Psychological Association in 1970 and 1971.
    1. Love—Congresses. I. Curtin, Mary Ellen, ed.
II. American Psychological Association.
[DNLM: 1. Love—Essays. BF575.L8 C978s 1973]
BF575.L8.S95   152.4   73-10475

Dedicated to my family, my teachers,
and to the unloved and unloving
MEC

Contents

Contributing Authors

ANNETTE M. BRODSKY, Ph. D.
Assistant Professor of Psychology
Department of Psychology and Psychological Clinic,
University of Alabama,Tuscaloosa, Alabama.

LAWRENCE, CASLER, Ph. D.
Professor of Psychology
Department of Psychology, State University College,
Geneseo, New York.

JAMES K. COLE, Ph. D.
Associate Professor of Psychology
Department of Psychology, University of Nebraska
Lincoln, Nebraska.

CHARLES CLAY DAHLBERG, M. D.
Fellow, Training, and Supervising Analyst; Research
Psychiatrist, William Alanson White Institute, New
York City; Associate Clinical Professor of Psychiatry
New York University Medical Center, New York
City; Assistant Visiting Neuropsychiatrist, Bellevue
Hospital Center, New York City.

ALBERT ELLIS, Ph. D.
Executive Director
Institute for Advanced Study in Rational Psycho-
therapy, New York City; Adjunct Professor of
Psychology, Union Graduate School, Antioch Col-
lege, Yellow Springs, Ohio.

SIDNEY M. GREENFIELD, Ph. D.
Professor of Sociology and Anthropology
Departments of Sociology and Anthropology,
The University of Wisconsin,Milwaukee, Wisconsin.

MARGARET M. HORTON, Ph. D.
Staff Psychologist
Malcolm Bliss Mental Health Center, St. Louis, Mo.
Adjunct Professor of Psychology
Department of Psychology, Lindenwood College
St. Louis, Missouri.

LOUIS J. KARMEL, Ph. D.
Professor of Counseling Psychology
School of Education, University of North Carolina
at Greensboro, Greensboro, North Carolina.

LEWIS R. LIEBERMAN, Ph. D.
Associate Professor of Psychology
Department of Psychology, Columbus College,
Columbus, Georgia.

SHIRLEY W. THOMAS, M. S.
Assistant Professor of Afro-American Studies
School of Afro-American Studies
California State University, San Diego, California.

EDITH WEIGERT, M. D.
Chairman of the Faculty
Washington School of Psychiatry, Washington, D. C.;
Supervising Analyst Washington Psychoanalytic
Institute, Washington, D. C.; Private Practice,
Psychiatry, Chevy Chase, Maryland.

ROGERS H. WRIGHT, Ph. D.
Private Practice, Psychology
Long Beach, California.

Preface

It has been said that "Love makes the world go 'round," yet not once did I see *love* mentioned in all 23 volumes in the indices of the *Annual Review of Psychology* under Emotion, Motivation, or Love itself. Is love sufficient or even necessary for the aforementioned great task and if so who talks about it besides poets and novelists and song writers?

The purpose of this book is to present a collection of serious essays about love. It considers how and in what ways love is important for individuals and groups, and if lacking, what kind of personal quality or interpersonal relation can adequately and rewardingly fill the void. The persons assembled for our symposium represent Psychology, Psychiatry, Anthropology, and Afro-American Studies.

These essays will be of interest to the general

reader who is curious about love in both usual and unusual kinds of situations. In addition, they may be helpful to persons for whom love, or the lack of it, is a problem and to those who try to help such persons.

I would like to mention here how our book came into being and to give credit to some persons for their contributions in the early part of the project. First was the appearance of Larry Casler's *Psychology Today* paper "This Thing Called Love Is Pathological" in December 1969. Larry "opened up the can of worms" for us. Then, a few months later, there was a conversation with Rogers Wright about topics for a symposium at a regional psychological association meeting. Rogers said he thought Larry's article would be an excellent starting point for a symposium that would look closely into a possible overemphasis on the necessity of love in our lives and, at the same time, explore a shrinking away from certain other troublesome personal qualities that might be molded into greater usefulness or made more serviceable in our lives, e.g., aggressiveness. It turned out that this topic was not used for a symposium at the regional meeting but one was organized and presented at the 1970 meeting of the American Psychological Association in Miami Beach. The third person I would like to thank is Sheldon Roen, psychologist and editor with Behavioral Publications, Inc., who heard the presentation at Miami Beach and suggested inviting additional papers on love with the idea of putting these in book form.

The next year another symposium on love took

place at the APA meeting, with second papers by some of the first symposium panel members and papers by two members of the Association for Women in Psychology, Annette Brodsky and Margaret Horton, who spoke, respectively, on special problems of love for women in therapy and a new kind of love, epigenetic love.

In addition to the symposium presentations by Casler and Wright, there were presentations both times by Sid Greenfield speaking from anthropological and economic viewpoints and by Lou Karmel always "making the case for love." Lew Lieberman, a discussant at the first APA, prepared general discussion comments for the book.

Completing the book are five invited papers on special topics: James Cole on homosexual love, Charles Dahlberg on sexual relationships between patient and therapist, Albert Ellis on what can be done about unhealthy love, Shirley Thomas on love in the Black experience, and Edith Weigert on love and respect.

To all of these people, I am grateful for the time and ideas invested in our book on love. Truly a labor for love.

One of my special hopes in exploring the subject of love was to find an acceptable substitute for persons for whom this kind of interpersonal relation (romantic love) is out of the question. It appears that our society, in large part, considers it important and necessary to the well-adjusted, "mature," and full life to love and be loved; consequently the unloved and unloving are made to feel as if they are incomplete persons. In this connection, it is heartening that the philosopher John Rawls has recently written that self-respect is perhaps the most important primary social good (*A Theory of Justice*, Harvard University Press, 1971). His definition of self-respect includes these aspects: (1) the person's sense of his own value and (2) confidence in one's ability to fulfill one's intentions. Is it possible that self-respect could be the acceptable substitute mentioned previously? To this end, in the present volume, Larry Casler suggests that social reformers might consider respect—for others, and above all, for self—as a better criterion than love for the truly mature person; and Edith Weigert writes of the importance of respect, as well as love, in creative human collaboration.

A number of friends have graciously helped with my editing chores. To these—Al P., Don D., Barbara R., Carolyn R., George L., Jim T., John C., Vince N., Natalie S.—and to others I must have forgotten, may I say, thank you.

Mary Ellen Curtin

Lexington, Kentucky
October 1972

1

Toward a Re-Evaluation of Love [1]

Lawrence Casler

LOVE HAS BEEN so pervasive a theme in philosophy and the creative arts for so long that one might almost regard it as an obsession. Sociologists, anthropologists, even archaeologists, have often attempted to penetrate the secret parts of this most compelling of emotions. It is strange, then, that psychology, the discipline most closely identified with the study of the emotions, has had so little to say on the topic. But this silence is now being broken.[2] The frontiers of psychological science are rapidly expanding, and current developments justify a fresh consideration of love at this time.

This essay will deal, primarily, with what is loosely termed romantic love. However, as will later be made explicit, many of the observations that follow are probably applicable to other varieties of love as well.

1

Love, like other emotions, can be examined in terms of its causes, its characteristics, and its consequences. Most of the early writings on the subject dealt chiefly with consequences, and led to such comforting but unenlightening—and perhaps untrue—conclusions as "love is good," or "necessary," or "healthy." Temporarily setting aside an inquiry into why or whether love makes life worth living, makes the world go 'round, and *vincit omnia*, let us first concern ourselves with the somewhat more manageable question of *causality* by asking why it is that people love.

There are many factors responsible for love between man and woman, but instinct is not one of them. Anthropologists have described entire societies in which love is absent[3], and there are certainly many individuals in our own love-oriented society who have never loved. To argue that such societies and such individuals are "sick" or "not quite human" or "the exception that proves the rule" is both unproductive and arrogantly ethnocentric. No, people have to learn to love, and they have to learn to want to love.[4] The reasons are not hard to find.

It seems safe to say that most people in our society need approval. Beset by parent-bred and competition-bred insecurity, we seek acceptance, confirmation, justification. Part of this need may be inescapable: life is a series of decisions, some trivial, some more substantial (coffee vs. tea, honesty vs. dishonesty, etc.). The mere fact that these *are* decisions implies the presence of uncertainty. And because most of us need to believe that we are right, we seek

2

external validation. This need may help to explain the rapture we feel when we meet someone who shares our preference for Palestrina, swimming, or crunchy peanut butter. (Likewise, the need for "validation" of our attitudes helps to explain why some of us so zealously attempt to change the attitudes of others, while some of these others display equal zeal in placing themselves in the orbit of strongly opinionated models. See Ausubel's [1970] discussion of "satellization.") Should we find one person whose choices in many different domains coincide with our own, we are likely to highly value this human buttress of our self- and world-concepts. And since that person's need for self-esteem is also being gratified, a reciprocal dependency develops.[5] The two individuals, so much like one another, begin to "like" one another. It is this attachment to a source of self-validation that provides, I believe, one of the foundations of love.

Note that the relationship between loving and being loved is a very intimate one. But this is not to say that a declaration of love automatically elicits a feeling of reciprocation. Indeed, it may lead to feelings of revulsion if the individual's self-image is already irretrievably low: "Anyone who says he loves *me* must be either a fool or a fraud." Still, in general, an individual is more likely to love a person from whom he perceives love. Indirect support for this generalization comes from a number of studies in which volunteer subjects are misled into believing that they are liked (or disliked) by other members of their group. This bit of misinformation is enough to elicit congruent feelings in the majority of the deceived subjects. A similar kind of feedback probably operates in the elaborate American game of dating. The young woman, for any of several reasons, may pretend to like her gentleman friend more than is actually the case. The gentleman, hungry for precisely this kind of response, responds favorably and in kind. And the poor woman, gratified by this expression of affection, now feels the fondness she had formerly feigned. Falling in love may thus be regarded, in cases such as these, as a snowball with a rotten core.

This line of reasoning may help to explain the fact that so many mama's boys, whose need for acceptance has been satisfied or satiated by maternal smother love, are apparently uninterested in seeking new romantic relationships.

But love is not simply a reaction to an ego-boost. We do not fall in love with everyone who shows a liking for us or for the things that we like. We have other needs that clamor for satisfaction. And the more needs that are satisfied by the same person, the greater becomes our tendency to love that person. One of the foremost of these other needs is called, very loosely, "sex." Accordingly, we can now somewhat refine our initial formulation: it is not simply the ego-booster who elicits our love; it is the ego-booster with sex appeal.

This statement contains some important implications. For example, the official mores of our society are such as to encourage us to seek sexual satisfaction only from a person with whom we have a pre-existing relationship (or, expressed more accurately, we are discouraged from seeking sexual satisfaction from anyone with whom we do *not* have a pre-existing relationship). Thus, the more ego-boosting a relationship is, the greater the tendency will be for the booster (at least the opposite-sexed booster) to serve—actually or potentially—as a sex-satisfier. Add to this tendency another tendency: sexual satisfaction from another is likely to provide ego satisfaction as well. Once again, the snowball effect is obvious.

While increasing numbers of people have liberated themselves from society's insistence that sexual intercourse occur only within the restrictive bonds of matrimony, the residue of early socialization may still remain. Even the relatively enlightened person may continue to feel that a purely sexual relationship is very impure indeed, and that sex unaccompanied by love is nasty, brutish, and not much fun. The only way for many sexually aroused individuals to avoid frustration, guilt, anxiety, and sin is to fall in love—and as quickly as possible. More declarations of love are probably uttered in parked cars than in any other single location. Some of these may be nothing more than seduction ploys,[6] but the likelihood is that self-seduction is involved in many cases. It is interesting that sex-play is often described as "making" (i.e., "creating") love.

We are indebted to Freud (1921) for the provocative hypothesis that love represents a sublimation of unacceptable sexual impulses. In any society that takes a dim view of sexuality, erotic impulses will be, he tells us, so anxiety-provoking that they will be

5

pushed out of consciousness. But to repress a need is not to destroy it. It continues to seek expression and eventually emerges in some other, more or less disguised, form. One such form may be love. To the extent that this theory is valid, we may conclude that an individual able to express his sexual needs directly might never fall in love. I shall return to this point later.

The psychoanalytic theory of love does not stop with the statement that sublimation is the principal mechanism. It proceeds to identify, quite precisely, the forbidden impulses that must be sublimated. The original impulses are predominantly incestuous (Freud, 1921). What every man wants is a girl just like the girl that married dear old Dad. The closer the resemblance (in age, name, temperament, physical appearance, etc.) between the loved one and the opposite-sexed parent, the greater the possibility that long-repressed incestuous tendencies will be reactivated. We thus have a rather neat explanation for at least some of the cases of impotence, frigidity, and wedding-night-turned-into-shambles that grace the pages of our clinical journals. Jean-Jacques Rousseau, who died more than a century before Freud's first work appeared, recounts his sexual initiation (which occurred at the age of twenty-one) with these words: "Was I happy? No; I tasted the pleasure, but I knew not what invincible sadness poisoned its charm. I felt as if I had committed incest. . . . " (quoted by Hunt, 1959, p. 256).

Unfortunately, rigorous testing of many psychoanalytic theories is extraordinarily difficult.

6

Some, including those just mentioned, simply do not seem to be susceptible to any experimental method yet devised. This is not to say that such formulations lack validity, but only that they lack the type of evidential support required for scientific acceptability.

The determinants of love that have been examined so far share a common factor: the molding force of society. The need for self-esteem certainly seems to be of social origin. And even the most skeptical non-Freudians (among whom the present writer counts himself) cannot deny that love in the Judaeo-Christian world would be a very different thing if there were no social regulations against free sex. Other social pressures—such as the love propaganda that infests television advertising—are perhaps of even greater causal significance. It is not surprising that we eventually stop thinking and simply internalize society's pro-love orientation. Most of us can no longer "choose" to love. Loving becomes something inevitable, like dying or getting married.

So thorough is the brain-washing that we may come to pity or scorn the person who is not in love. The pity or scorn may, of course, be self-directed, but not for long: a person who does not have the inner resources to stand alone can usually impose himself upon someone who is equally incapacitated.

Besides being love-oriented, ours is a marriage-oriented society. From early childhood on, we hear countless statements beginning, "When (not *if*) you get married . . . " And, just as love is regarded as a necessary prerequisite for sex, it is regarded as a necessary prerequisite for marriage. People still seem to believe that love and marriage go together like a horse and carriage, apparently without acknowledging that horses and carriages have not gone together for many years.[7] As a result, the insecurity and the fear of social punishment that propel most of us into marriage serve also to provide extremely powerful motives for falling in love.

Love, then, may be viewed as a consequence of the needs for self-esteem, sexual satisfaction, and conformity to social pressures. From this perspective, love loses its uniqueness and, therefore, some of its halo. Hatred, too, may reflect the need for self-esteem and may have a strong sexual component; and it may even, in societies that are as aggression-oriented as ours is love-oriented, be instigated by social pressures. So to state that love is, somehow, intrinsically a superior emotion is to express a current cultural bias. Nothing is good or bad but culture makes it so.

While the *causes* of love are not essentially different from those of many other emotional states, its *characteristics* do separate it from the other emotions. Several of the emotions are characterized by specific and distinguishable biochemical reactions and can be activated by operations performed on fairly circumscribed portions of the anatomy. Anger, for example, can be inferred quite reliably from adrenal and other secretions, and its control can be traced to particular parts of the hypothalamus.[8] However, no physiological indices have been discovered for love.[9] This failure can be explained in a number of ways. Perhaps there is no biological correlate of this particular emotion, due to the fact that no particular behavioral response (such as flight, in the case of fear) provides any evolutionary advantage. Perhaps there *is* a correlate, but one so subtle that it has not yet been observed. Or perhaps the emotion of love is really a composite of more basic emotional states, the physiological effects of which cancel each other out.

This last possibility seems especially worthy of consideration. Let us assume that love is directed toward a person who makes us "happy" or satisfies many of our needs. Physiological studies suggest that need-satisfaction typically is associated (either as a cause or an effect) with physical relaxation. And yet physical relaxation does not appear to be a usual concomitant of love. Is it not possible that the relaxation provided by need-satisfaction is being neutralized by sexual arousal or by such other tension-producing emotions as anger or fear? The intrusion of either of these latter emotions should not occasion surprise. The lover may well be angry because he resents becoming increasingly dependent upon another person. (Recall that the loved person is likely to be viewed as the actual or potential gratifier of more and more needs and therefore becomes more and more indispensable.) A man can develop strong negative feelings toward his mistress or his wife just as he can develop strong negative feelings toward the cigarettes or the race track to which he is addicted.

Another likely accompaniment of need-satisfaction is fear. Every increase in dependency increases the fear of losing the source of gratification.[10] There is always the chance of loss through death; but the feared loss is more usually based, at least in competitive societies, on the possibility that the loved one will find someone else more gratifying. The fear of loss of another person is thus fused with the fear of loss of self-esteem. So the emotion of love, based in part on dependency and the desire for ego-enhancement, is characterized, almost from the beginning, by anger and fear. And this ugly combination of anger and fear, which is probably what we mean by "jealousy," may take out of the relationship most of the satisfaction upon which it was built.

While both fear and anger seem to be intimately involved in love, fear is probably the more fundamental of these, inasmuch as anger may be viewed as a reaction to fear.[11] Based on the foregoing considerations, a working definition of love finally emerges: love is the fear of losing an important source of need gratification. As a corollary, we may add that the fear increases as a function of the importance and the number of needs that are involved in the relationship. The romantic effusion, "I can't live without you," may thus be understood as an expression of almost paralyzing panic. The feared loss of the loved one becomes equated with the feared loss of self. And the outcome of the equation may well be suicide.

The definition proposed here differs markedly from a number of others that have gained wide acceptance. The trouble with such uplifting definitions as, "Love is that condition in which the happiness of another person is essential to your own," (Heinlein, 1961, p. 345) is that they suffer from incompleteness. *Why* is the other person's happiness essential? I suggest that the answer is, quite simply, that a partner who is not happy is likely to terminate the relationship. Fear thus remains the more fundamental explanation.[12]

Up to now, my emphasis has been on the man-woman kind of love. But the same four-letter word is used in an almost infinite variety of other contexts. Besides loving his wife or girl friend, one may love his parents, his children, children in general, his country, Beethoven's Ninth, gin rummy, sunsets, the New York Mets, and God. (We shall return to God later.) Hopefully, the emotion is somewhat different in each of these cases, but there is considerable overlap as well. Thus, while the emphasis in these pages will continue to be on only one type of love, parts of the analysis will be of obvious relevance to the other varieties as well (including the love of love that seems to afflict so many psychotherapists, preachers, and adolescents of all ages[13]). For example, whatever is loved is likely to be a potent satisfier of multiple needs. A person loves a painting not only because of the aesthetic pleasure it provides, but also because of the other needs (such as the need for status) that are being concurrently satisfied. But, as has already been stressed, need-satisfaction is not enough. Only those experiences that are felt to be transitory can inspire love. It is probably easier to love a painting

11

that hangs on a museum wall than one that can be seen every day in the living room.[14]

Another way in which the various kinds of love are related has to do with the fact that we know a great deal about a person if we know what he loves. There is a difference between the man who loves to drink sherry and the man who loves to drink, just as there is a difference between the woman who loves her teen-aged son and the woman who loves teen-aged boys.

One very important characteristic shared by many types of love is the primacy of tactile contact. The mother wishes to touch her child almost constantly; young lovers are obsessed by the desire for physical contact; puppies are petted; and the vain person (the lover of self) continually engages in hair-patting and other self-touching activity. Even the rhesus monkeys in Harlow's well-known experiments (Harlow, 1958) provide evidence that whatever love may be, it is likely to be found in the presence of something soft and cuddly.

One explanation for the potency of tactile stimulation is that the skin is so richly endowed with nerve endings. Neurophysiologists have found, further, that the nerve fibers connecting the skin and the central nervous system are better developed at birth than are the fibres from any of the other organs. Most experiences of the newborn infant are, therefore, tactile. His first contact with his mother is skin contact, and, as the other modes of receptivity develop, these may be associated with cutaneous

12

stimulation. For example, if the baby is held during feeding, skin contact will probably become associated with the satisfaction of hunger. Touching another person acquires linkages with an expanding number of needs and finally reaches the status of an independent source of gratification. There thus appears to be a progression: from *skin* love, to *kin* love, to *in* love. It is no accident that lovers are so fond of kissing (the mouth is particularly well supplied with nerve endings), or that when love finds its ultimate physical expression in sexual intercourse, more square inches of skin receive stimulation than in any other conceivable joint activity. Undeniably, romance is often a touching experience. It was Sebastien Chamfort who, in the eighteenth century, observed that love was only "the contact of two epidermises" (quoted in Hunt, 1959, p. 256). Recent research in the psychology of imagery lends support to Chamfort's contention. When college students are asked to describe their reactions to the word "love," they regularly refer to "a member of the opposite sex in relatively close physical contact" (Bugelski, 1970, p. 1011).

Still, love is more than skin deep. If we examine the language of love, we find unmistakable intimations of yet another component of this complex emotion. At varying levels of discourse, we encounter such verbal descriptions of the experience or the expression of love as "adoration," "heavenly transport," and "soul kiss." The loved one is called an angel, a goddess, a divine creature. Perhaps the most

13

seminal assertion in the entire Bible is that "God is love." In the poetry of Dante Gabriel Rossetti ("The House of Life") appear the lines,

Lady, I fain would tell how evermore
Thy soul I know not from thy body, nor
Thee from myself, neither our love from God.

In short, the interpenetration of love and religion is too pervasive to be regarded as either accidental or incidental.

The worship of the beloved, along with many other features of "romantic love," can be traced to practices and principles first made explicit during the era of courtly love. In his brilliant chronicle, *The Natural History of Love*, Morton Hunt (1959, pp. 151, 165, 166) provides several cases in point. The lady of the troubadours (who was often addressed as "Madonna") was an "inert, icon-like figure." A biographer of Duke Louis of Bourbon described him as "a very amorous knight, first towards God and then towards all ladies and highborn girls." And one writer of the period, we are told, "had the temerity to portray Lancelot coming to Guinevere's room . . . and then bowing and genuflecting at her door as he leaves, precisely as if before a shrine."

Perhaps the ubiquitous and apparently unceasing influence of courtly love can best be understood in terms of this trinity of love, sex, and religion. The linkage of the three has received particularly vivid

14

documentation in religious writings. St. Theresa of Avila (quoted in Leuba, 1924, p. 364) offers this description of a visionary experience:

> I saw an angel close by me, on my left side, in bodily form. . . . He was not large, but small of stature and most beautiful—his face burning as if he were one of the highest angels, who seem to be all of fire. . . . I saw in his hand a long spear of gold, and at the iron's point there seemed to be a little fire. He appeared to me to be thrusting it at times into my heart, and to pierce my very bowels: when he drew it out, he seemed to draw them out also and to leave me all on fire with a great love of God. The pain was so great that I cried out, but at the same time the sweetness which that violent pain gave me was so excessive that I could not wish to be rid of it. . . . [15]

This does not seem much different from the plea to "sheath in my heart sharp pain up to the hilt," in a love poem by Coventry Patmore (quoted by Hunt, *op. cit.*, p. 326), nor the phallic "sheathings" and "thrustings" that loom so large in the avid descriptions of Fanny Hill.[16]

The investiture of nuns is, in essence, a wedding ceremony; a nun who has sexual intercourse is

15

regarded as an adulteress. Moreover, many of the non-Christian religions have similar erotic attributes.[17]

A few words, and this part of the analysis will be complete. If a statistical analysis of the contents of works of art were to be conducted, two themes would surely predominate. Recurring again and again, across centuries, national boundaries, styles, and artistic modalities, are Eros and Thanatos—love and death. Frequently, the two are inextricably linked. One need only consider Michelangelo's early rendering of the "Pietà" to be struck by the juxtaposition of sensuous love and the finality of death. In music, perhaps the ultimate expression of this fusion is Wagner's "Liebestod" (love-death). In literature, a recent analysis of the short stories of W. Somerset Maugham reveals "a significant relationship between love and death at the 5% level, by a Chi-square test" (Judson, 1963). People have been "embracing death" since at least 1603.[18] In the vivid language of Rollo May (1968), "Death is always in the shadow of the delight of love."[19] And an early commentator has pointed out the close relationship in Platonic thought between the emotion of love and the desire for immortality (Alles, 1933).[20]

The mediating role of sexuality should not be overlooked. Many have described the "Liebestod" as an orgasm set to music. The French refer to sexual climax as "la petite mort." Mere metaphors? Perhaps. But sacred and profane love may well be regarded as the twin offspring of sex and the fear of death.

16

This exploration of the characteristics of love has led us dangerously close to the quicksands of metaphysics. Let us avert the further temptations of free association by simply concluding that love is a unique emotion only because it uniquely combines a number of other potent emotional states. "Pure" love, unalloyed by other emotions, probably does not exist.

Fortunately, a consideration of the *consequences* of love can be both safer and shorter. It can be safer, because there are fewer philosophical booby traps. (Plato did say that by loving a beautiful person, one comes to know God; but his arguments, including his specific advocacy of homosexuality, no longer seem particularly cogent.) And the consideration can be relatively brief because of the close relationship between the consequences of love and many of the causes already discussed. Thus, being in love permits one to have guilt-free sex, to marry, and to have the self-concept of a normal, healthy citizen of the Western World.

Love also has a tendency to cause alterations in psychological processes. According to a charming statement that I have been able to trace back no further than its utterance in an old movie called "Mr. Skeffington," "A woman is beautiful only when she is loved." The statement is not quite accurate. A woman (likewise a chair, a worm, a grain of sand) may become beautiful when the perceiver has been primed with LSD, alcohol, hypnosis, or anything else that can induce hallucinations. While not strikingly original, the conclusion cannot be avoided that love

17

may lead to the delusion of overevaluation. I am not referring here to the respect that every person owes his fellows nor to the gratitude felt for services rendered, but rather to the fawning, slobbering idolatry that lovers have displayed, on and off, since the eleventh century. The doting lover is doomed either to painful disillusion or to the permanent delusion that so closely resembles psychosis. And the person doted upon must either play the exalted role that he or she has been assigned or risk the termination of the relationship. There is no fall quite so precipitous as the fall from grace of an overvalued lover. Love, therefore, may bring forth fraud.

Some may argue that I am speaking here only of immature infatuation, rather than of the true love that does not alter when it alteration finds. Mature love, they may insist, is a broadening, deepening experience—perhaps the most enriching experience a human being can have. This postulation of the salutary effects of love is so pervasive that we must examine its validity. First, of course, there is the matter of evidence. Subjective reports are notoriously unreliable, and experimental studies are, at present, out of the question. To state that a love relationship causes one to mature is rather empty unless we know that the individual would not have matured just as readily in the absence of love. There is no evidence that love is either necessary or sufficient for psychological maturity. Indeed, to the extent that love fosters dependency, it may well be a deterrent to maturity. Perhaps the most that can be said is that in a love-oriented society, being in love assuages feelings of insecurity so that the individual is more likely to be able to develop his potentialities. The feelings of satisfaction generated by love may be misleading, akin to the satisfaction afforded to an addict by a drug.

It should be clear that I am not saying that the effects of love always border on the pathological.[21] It is not love but the *need* for love that may be pathological, just as it is the need to use a crutch rather than the crutch itself that signifies physical incapacity. The person who seeks love in order to strengthen his self-respect will become, in the style of the alcoholic, increasingly dependent on this illusory source of well-being. The truly mature person who seeks love would probably not trap himself in this way. But would the mature person seek love at all? Let us attempt an answer to this rather tantalizing question.

I think we can say that the nonloving person in our society is likely to be in a state of either very good or very bad mental health. The latter possibility probably requires no extended explanation. One of the standard stigmata of emotional disturbance is the inability to love. Many varieties of psychotherapy have as their primary goal the fostering of this ability. Some therapies go so far as to designate the therapist himself as a proper recipient of the patient's newly released love impulses (perhaps on the assumption that if the patient can love his therapist, he can love anybody).

The other part of the statement—that a love-free person may be in excellent mental health—may seem

19

less acceptable. But if the need for a love relationship is based largely on insecurity, conformity to social pressures, and sexual frustration, then the person who is secure, independent, and has a satisfactory sex life—i.e., the person who has reached adulthood without becoming psychologically crippled—will not need to love. He may *enjoy* loving and being loved, but he will not *need* these experiences. He will not be one of those forlorn people who feel incomplete except when romantically entangled. He will, rather, be a person who does not find his own company boring—a person whose inner resources are such that other people, while providing pleasure and stimulation, cease to be absolutely necessary. We have long been enjoined to love others as we love ourselves. But perhaps we seek love relationships with others only because we do not sufficiently love ourselves.

What would a healthy love-free person be like? We might assume that "coldness" would be among his most salient characteristics. But "coldness" is a relative term. A "cold" person is simply one who does not give us the "warmth" we want or need. The attribution of "coldness" thus tells us at least as much about the person doing the attributing as it does about the person who is thus characterized. Absence of warmth is responded to negatively only by those dependent persons who interpret it as rejection. (In a similar vein, a nymphomaniac has been defined as a woman whose sex drive is stronger than that of the person who is calling her a nymphomaniac.)

Would the love-free person be egocentric?

Perhaps, but only if that term is relieved of its ugly connotations. To be "self-centered" does not mean to disregard the worth of other people, but only to react to them within a frame of reference that is centered on the self. There is nothing reprehensible about this manner of reacting. In fact, most psychologists would probably accept the position that we are *all* inescapably self-centered. No matter how other-directed our activities may appear to be, they are functions of *our* perception of the world (based, in turn, on *our* previous experiences) and may have little to do with what is really "out there." Since every act is thus a "self-ish" one, evaluative criteria can only be applied to the effects of selfishness, rather than to selfishness *per se*.

One obstacle that blocks acceptance of the position being presented here is our previous experience with people who are nonloving. Such individuals are typically arrogant, cruel, and/or frightened. But these people, I suggest, have not freed themselves from the need to love; on the contrary, their psychological difficulties have rendered them incapable of love. The coldness they display may rightly be interpreted as a form of defensiveness that serves to keep distance between themselves and others. For such people, closeness is intolerable. By nearly every criterion of mental health, these nonlovers need help. They differ markedly from those nonlovers for whom emotional closeness may be pleasurable without being necessary for the enjoyment of life.

In recent years, an increasing number of authors have extolled, sometimes with great eloquence, the

21

emotion of love. The absence of love, they claim, is what causes wars, emotional breakdowns, and most of mankind's other woes. While it may be unfair to demand that these writers provide evidence to support their contentions, it should be pointed out that the value of love remains to be demonstrated.[22] Perhaps the goal of social reformers should be not love but *respect*—respect for others and, most of all, for oneself.

The purpose of this section of the essay has not been anti-love, but pro-people. To love a person means, all too often, to use that person. And exploitation, even when it is mutual, is incompatible with whatever we mean by human growth. Our society's current emphasis on love is, I believe, both an effect and a cause of the insecurity, the dependency, and the absence of self-respect that may some day be the death of us all. Perhaps this thought is behind Arthur Koestler's recent comment, "We are thus driven to the unfashionable and uncomfortable conclusion that the trouble with our species is not an overdose of self-asserting *aggression*, but an excess of self-transcending *devotion*" (1969, p. 112). Like a crutch, love may (when its causes and characteristics are such as to justify referring to it as a "need") have the consequence of impending the exercise of our potential for growth. And whatever inhibits growth tends to be self-perpetuating.

The overemphasis on love is not, of course, the only form of "crutch-ification" that may be contributing to the atrophy of human dignity. Any personal fetish or stagnant social institution can have

22

the same effect. Marriage, for example, may currently be doing at least as much harm as good. The various religions, too, are obvious candidates for analysis in these terms. But it is the idea of the value of love that has been accepted most uncritically and is, therefore, most deserving of careful scrutiny at this time.

I would like to conclude by examining some of the implications of the idea that love has become vastly overvalued in our society. There are three social phenomena especially worthy of discussion—child-rearing practices, the institution of marriage, and the current attempts to eliminate sexual discrimination against women—each intimately related to the other two, and each related, quite directly, to the ways in which society views love.

In the first place, our present love orientation has invaded the nursery. Most laymen and, for that matter, most psychologists are firmly convinced that young children need to be loved if they are to develop properly. On what basis is this assertion made? Certainly not on the basis of evidence. The evidence that is usually cited (Bowlby, 1951; Spitz, 1945; etc.) is so vulnerable to criticism that it would be rejected at once if it dealt with a less emotion-laden topic. As I have indicated elsewhere (Casler, 1968), there is simply no good evidence that human infants, or the young of any other species, need to be loved in order to attain an optimal level of development. The adherence to this myth can be explained, I think, rather simply by the prevailing deification of love in our society, and by the fact that

23

most adults in our society probably do need love and project this need into the next generation. It is undoubtedly true that people who have become accustomed to love are likely to suffer when the love is withdrawn. Analogous withdrawal symptoms appear when drug addicts are deprived of drugs. By what kind of logic does the existence of withdrawal symptoms prove that love is a necessity while drug addiction is a nasty habit?

Some readers may believe that the person who never experiences love as a child will be unable to experience love as an adult. There are three answers to this argument. First, there is evidence against it: many individuals who have been brought up in relatively impersonal institutional settings do fall in love, get married, etc. Second, the objection presupposes that the adult form of love is very similar to the childhood form; but the kind of love that goes on between the child and his mother is based almost entirely on the dependency of the child and the inequality in status between child and mother—certainly not the kind of love that any of us want to perpetuate among adults. The third answer to the argument that children without love will become adults without love is, "So what?" As I have been attempting to point out, an adult without love can be happy, emotionally fulfilled, and socially useful.

Children do have needs that go beyond those necessary for physical survival: properly timed and modulated sensory stimulation, experience with language, and exposure to adults and other children who can provide models of, and reinforcements for, appropriate behavior. But all of these needs can be satisfied outside of a family setting. As Jacob Gewirtz has commented, "Institutions can be engineered to provide relatively good environments for children, while a family may provide a relatively poor caretaking environment" (1968, p. 200). Other writers go much further. "One sometimes wonders," wrote Norman Haire, "whether the average parents are not the least fit persons in the world to bring up their own child" (quoted in Westermarck, 1937, p. 159). In a similar vein, Schmalhausen commented, "Are parents to be pitied? Yes, I think so. Pitied and shot" (1930, p. 293).

If it is true that children can thrive in the absence of love, this fact would have far-reaching ramifications for our entire family structure. Marriage and the nuclear family undoubtedly fulfilled many important individual and social functions in times past: economic, sexual, religious, and other pressures combined to make marriage, for most people, a useful and/or desirable institution. But most of the presumed original functions of marriage are now being satisfied in nonmarital arrangements, and social theorists have been proclaiming, either optimistically or pessimistically, that marriage is becoming obsolete. The objection usually raised against this prediction or proclamation of obsolescence has been that marriage is essential because children need to be brought up lovingly, within a family setting. But if, as I have been suggesting, this claim is invalid—if children can be brought up quite satisfactorily in the absence of parents or affectionate parent-substitutes, then this last justification for society's insistence on marriage is itself obsolete. I am not, of course, advocating the abolition of marriage, such a step being highly impractical at the present time. What I do invite you to consider is that other forms of relationships might be socially acceptable alternatives for those who desire them, with no prescriptions as to the duration of the relationship or the number of partners permitted. (For further comments on contemporary marriage, see Casler, 1970.)

These comments concerning child-rearing and the value of marriage lead inescapably to a consideration of women's rights. The glorification of motherhood and the sanctification of marriage have been, along with the mystification of romantic love, chiefly responsible for the centuries-old suppression of women. As long as marriage and family living are viewed as individual and social necessities, women are likely to find themselves (willingly or not) forced into domesticity or into second-class status in the outside world. A woman's place will be in the home as long as "the home" is regarded with reverence and is defined in terms of nurturance and love. In former times, this husbandry of women was referred to as the "three K's" (*Kinder, Kirche,* and *Küche*). Although it may now have evolved into what might be called the "three F's" (feeding, flattering, and having sexual intercourse),[23] the fact remains that marriage can be de-individualizing and de-humanizing. Both partners run the risk of being infected, but there are good reasons for believing

26

that the risk is substantially greater for women. To quote Simone de Beauvoir, "It has been said that marriage diminishes man, which is often true; but almost always it annihilates woman" (1961, p. 450).

The Women's Liberation movement probably poses the most serious threat to marriage that has ever been mounted. It is bound to be more effective than the occasional male protestations against the anachronistic institution. After all, marriage may well have been invented by women, bartering their bodies for economic security, and it is women who have been matrimony's most zealous defenders. But it appears that women are beginning to grow tired of having to give up their autonomy, their freedom of movement, even their names, in order to establish a socially approved relationship, just as they have grown tired of being deprived of equal economic opportunities, and just as they have grown tired of being viewed, and perhaps even viewing themselves, as little more than vaginas with legs.

Thus, a benign circle may be in the process of developing. As women become more liberated, the bonds of domesticity will weaken; and as these bonds weaken, women will become free. And behind this evolutionary progression, there must be, I believe, a corresponding devaluation of the emotion of love. The only answer to the question, "Love: who needs it?" is this: most people in our society need love, but the situation may be improving.

FOOTNOTES

1. This chapter is an expanded version of papers presented before the American Psychological Association in Miami Beach, Florida, on September 4, 1970, and in Washington, D. C., on September 5, 1971. An earlier version appeared in the December, 1969, issue of *Psychology Today*.

2. There are still a few, particularly of the Freudian persuasion, who believe that love cannot and should not be examined within a scientific perspective (see, for example, Karmel's papers in this volume). This contention can best be rebutted, perhaps, by another representative of the psychoanalytic point of view: "It is inevitable, therefore, that science should lay hands on the stuff which poets have fashioned so as to give pleasure to mankind for thousands of years, although its touch must be clumsier and the result in pleasure less. These considerations may serve to vindicate our handling of the loves of men and women as well as other things in a strictly scientific way. For science betokens the most complete renunciation of the pleasure-principle of which our minds are capable." If these words by Freud (1910, pp. 192-193) are to be taken seriously, the scientific method appears to be the most mature method by which the emotion of love can be studied.

3. There is at least one society, the Manu of New Guinea, that has no word for "love" in its language (see Frumkin, 1961).

4. This point was made by one of the other con-

tributors to this volume more than two decades ago (Ellis, 1949). Cf. Waller's characterization of love as a "bad habit" (1951, p. 119). For an interesting presentation of the opposing point of view, that the need for love is "instinctoid," see Maslow (1965).

5. "Love might be analyzed as the mutual tendency of two individuals to reinforce each other" (Skinner, 1953, p. 310).

6. A folk-saying of unknown origin asserts that the way to a woman's genitals is through her heart, while the way to a man's heart is through his genitals.

7. It is interesting to note, in this connection, that courtly love—from which romantic love probably descends—was distinctly separate from courtly marriage. "Love and marriage are two intentions that go by separate and distinct roads" (Montaigne, in Frame, 1967, p. 649. Orig. pub. 1585-1588).

8. In an important paper, Schachter and Singer (1962) present a contrary hypothesis.

9. According to recent rumors, love may have its home in the parasympathetic branch of the autonomic nervous system, or in the septum (for information concerning this latter possibility, consult Heath, 1964). But these localizations have received, as yet, little more substantiation than earlier ones in the heart, the liver, or the groin.

10. "Security seems to be a function of not only the extent to which one's needs are met at the present but also the extent to which they will probably be met in the future" (Thamm, unpub., p. 1). Cf. Montaigne's comment that "in love there is nothing but

a frantic desire for what flees from us" (in Frame, 1967, p. 137. Orig, pub. 1572-1580).

11. According to Bowlby, "threat of loss of a partner arouses anxiety and actual loss causes sorrow, while both situations are likely to arouse anger" (1968, p. 96). This formulation deals very largely with observable variables and is congruent with the position being taken here. Fraiberg thus appears to have been incorrect in asserting that "the behaviorists cannot well explain . . . the admixture of aggression in the most sublime love" (1967, p. 48).

12. It may be useful to consider the following example. An individual returns home from a convention and is greeted by the question, "Did you enjoy yourself, Dear?" He replies, "Yes, as a matter of fact, I did. I met this very attractive person there, and we ended up going to bed together." Now, the loving response to this report would be, by some definitions, "Oh, I'm so glad. I hope you had fun." But is this the response you are likely to get? Hardly. More likely, the ensuing anger, tears, or threats will be enough to cause you to refrain from repeating—or at least from reporting—such behaviors in the future. If love is the altruistic emotion it is supposed to be, then why the anger, the tears, the threats? The argument that the person who reacts in this fashion is not "really" in love is unrealistic, reflecting a conception of what love should be, rather than what it actually is, as experienced by those who claim they are in love. The outraged feelings of the aggrieved partner in the foregoing example are, I suggest, expressions of a thwarted pro-

prietorship that reflects a fear of competition that ultimately stems from a fear of loss.

13. The near equivalence of one's attachment to a love object and one's attachment to the attachment was made explicit as long ago as 1937, by Ernest Jones: "What is most precious to the person may be equally described as tenderness towards an object or the object itself" (p. 2).

14. Likewise, "love of life" would probably be nonexistent in the absence of our perception of our own mortality.

15. As might be expected, a male saint provides a somewhat different perspective: "Even so our dear Lord offers the breast of his divine love to the devout soul; he draws, gathers it into the lap of his more than motherly tenderness, and then, burning with love, he embraces the soul, presses it to his heart, kisses it with the sacred kisses of his mouth, makes it taste of that love which is better than wine. And so the soul, intoxicated with delight, not merely consents and yields to the divine union, but cooperates with all its might thereto" (St. François de Sales, quoted in Tarachow, 1960, p. 545).

16. Leuba, *op. cit.*, after quoting several similar accounts of mystical experiences, concludes, "We must surrender to the evidence. . . . [These authors] suffer from nothing else than intense attacks of erotomania, induced by their organic need and the worship of the God of love" (p. 370).

17. Note should be made, however, of de Beauvoir's comment that "it is not that mystical love has a sexual character, but that the sexuality of the

woman in love is tinged with mysticism" (1961, p. 610).

18. "Martyrs . . . did most willingly embrace their deaths" (Crosse, 1603).

19. Freud had earlier speculated that the Goddess of Love had once been identical to the Goddess of Death (1913). Note, too, the familiar legend of the Sirens who used erotic lures to bring men to destruction. (See, in this connection, Putnam's brief note [1970], aptly titled "Love and Death.")

20. Cf. this quotation from Plato's Symposium: "Eros . . . is intermediate between the divine and the mortal. He is the mediator between men and gods, and therefore in him all is bound together."

21. The title of my 1969 article, "This Thing Called Love is Pathological," was added by an editor and does not accurately reflect my position.

22. Some apparently believe that such demonstration is already available. Many of the communications received following earlier presentations of these ideas indicated unsuspected similarities between members of "hippie" society and their arch-conservative elders. A sizable proportion of each group seems to be possessed by a near-fanatical enthusiasm for love. (Both groups, too, appear to have members quite capable of writing hate-mail to persons who do not share their enthusiasm.)

23. See Cantarow, et al., 1970.

Toward a Re-Evaluation of Love

REFERENCES

Alles, A. Platonic love. *Psychological Bulletin*, 1933, *30*, 611-612.

Ausubel, D. *Theory and problems in child development.* (2nd ed.). New York: Grune and Stratton, 1970.

Bowlby, J. *Maternal care and mental health.* Geneva: WHO Monograph Series, No. 2, 1951.

Bowlby, J. Effects on behavior of disruption of an affectional bond. In J. M. Thoday and A. S. Pardes (Eds.), *Genetic and environmental influences on behavior.* New York: Plenum Press, 1968.

Bugelski, B. Words and things and images. *American Psychologist*, 1970, *25*, 1002-1012.

Cantarow, E., Diggs, E., Ellis, K., Marx, J., Robinson, L., and Schein, M. On women's liberation. In H. Gadlin and B. Gerskof (Eds.), *The uptight society: A book of readings.* Belmont, California: Brooks-Cole, 1970.

Casler. L. Perceptual deprivation in institutional settings. In G. Newton and S. Levine (Eds.), *Early experience and behavior.* Springfield, Illinois: Charles C. Thomas, 1968.

Casler, L. This thing called love is pathological. *Psychology Today*, 1969, *3* (7), 18, ff.

Casler, L. Marriage motives in two college populations. *Personality*, 1970, *1*, 221-229.

Crosse, H. *Vertues common-wealth.* London, 1603.

de Beauvoir, S. *The second sex.* New York: Bantam Books, 1961.

Ellis, A. Some significant correlates of love and fam-

33

ily attitudes and behavior. *Journal of Social Psychology*, 1949, *30*, 3-16.

Fraiberg, S. The origins of human bonds. *Commentary*, 1967, *44* (6), 47-58.

Frame, D. *Complete works of Montaigne*. Stanford: Stanford University Press, 1967.

Freud, S. *Contributions to the psychology of love: A special type of object choice made by man*. New York: Basic Books, 1959. (Orig. pub., 1910).

Freud, S. *The theme of the three caskets*. New York: Basic Books, 1959. (Orig. pub., 1913).

Freud, S. *Group psychology and the analysis of the ego*. London: Hogarth Press, 1955. (Orig. pub., 1921).

Frumkin, R. Sexual freedom. In A. Ellis and A. Abarbanel (Eds.), *The encyclopedia of sexual behavior*. New York: Hawthorn, 1961.

Gewirtz, J. On designing the functional environment of the child to facilitate behavioral development. In L. Dittmann (Ed.), *New perspectives in early child care*. New York: Atherton, 1968.

Harlow, H. The nature of love. *American Psychologist*, 1958, *13*, 673-685.

Heath, R. Pleasure response of human subjects to direct stimulation of the brain. In R. Heath (Ed.), *The role of pleasure in behavior*. New York: Harper and Row, 1964.

Heinlein, R. *Stranger in a strange land*. New York: Putnam, 1961.

Hunt, M. *The natural history of love*. New York: Knopf, 1959.

Jones, E. Love and morality: A study in character

types. *International Journal of Psycho-analysis*, 1937, *18*, 1-5.

Judson, A. Love and death in the short stories of W. Somerset Maugham: A psychological analysis. *Psychiatric Quarterly Supplement*, 1963, *37*, 250-262.

Koestler, A. Man—one of evolution's mistakes? *New York Times Magazine*, October 19, 1969, 28 ff.

Leuba, J. The sex impulse in Christian mysticism. *Journal of Abnormal and Social Psychology*, 1924, *19*, 357-372.

Maslow, A. Criteria for judging needs to be instinctoid. In M. Jones (Ed.), *Human motivation: A symposium*. Lincoln: University of Nebraska Press, 1965.

May, R. The daemonic: Love and death. *Psychology Today*, 1968, *1* (9), 16-25.

Putnam, M. Horace, Carm. 1.5: Love and death. *Classical Philology*, 1970, *65*, 251-254.

Schachter, S., and Singer, J. Cognitive, social, and physiological determinants of emotional state. *Psychological Review*, 1962, *69*, 379-399.

Schmalhausen, S. Family life: A study in pathology. In F. Calverton and S. Schmalhausen (Eds.), *The new generation*. New York: Macaulay, 1930.

Skinner, B. F. *Science and human behavior*. New York: Macmillan, 1953.

Spitz, R. Hospitalism: An inquiry into the genesis of psychiatric conditions in early childhood. *Psychoanalytic Study of the Child*, 1945, *1*, 53-74.

Tarachow, S. Judas, the beloved executioner. *Psychoanalytic Quarterly*, 1960, *29*, 528-554.

Thamm, R. The distribution of interpersonal involvement: A humanistic theory. Unpublished, n.d.

Waller, W., and Hill, R. *The family—A dynamic interpretation*. New York: Dryden, 1951.

Westermarck, E. *The future of marriage in western civilization*. New York: Macmillan, 1937.

2

I. Love: Some Reflections by a Social Anthropologist

Sidney M. Greenfield

THE OBJECTIVE OF this paper is to examine the attitudinal-behavioral configuration referred to as love from the structural-functional perspective of social anthropology and to project from that analysis some implications for current discussions of social change. This in itself is somewhat novel. The overwhelming number of efforts to treat love from a scientific perspective have been made by psychologists. I, however, am not a psychologist and I admit my limited knowledge of the field. As a social anthropologist, my analysis shall proceed, of course, from the perspective of my discipline.

Social anthropologists generally focus their research and investigations on the shared, repetitive, and regularly patterned aspects of human social existence. They then examine these cultural behaviors in terms of their larger social and cultural contexts, seeking to explain them in terms of both their origin and function. Hence, social anthropology is not interested in all aspects of human behavior, but rather in those behaviors repetitively performed by the members of a society or a social group in specific social situations.

To anyone who has studied or is familiar with American society, love is a term that may be meaningfully applied to an observable, repetitive, and patterned set of behaviors. Americans of all ages "fall in love" and enough has been written on the subject that the reader need not be burdened with the all too familiar details.

Most students of anthropology, however, have come from and/or have been trained in the United States or Great Britain. When they went off to study other peoples and their cultures (primitive, tribal, peasant, and contemporary), they generally were familiar with the behavior, associated attitudes, and emotional states to which the term love referred. What they found was that in some cultures people, particularly those participating in a mating relationship, shared strong emotional ties and behaved as did people in love back in the United States and Europe. In other cultures, however, there was little in either the behavior, emotional states, or attitudes of people that could in the most remote way be compared to love in the western world. In still other societies, people manifested the behavioral syndrome and the emotions called love, but were treated in ways ranging from benign neglect to being considered hopelessly insane and at times dangerous and therefore to be removed from social participation.

The behavioral pattern then, so important and apparently "natural" to persons raised and socialized in Europe and America, turns out not to be innate and universal, but, rather, limited to a specific range of societies. In those societies, the pattern makes a demonstrable contribution to the working of the total social system. Considerable variability, however, is to be observed in both behavior and associated attitudes from society to society within the class in which the pattern has been institutionalized, and within single societies between social segments or groups. In comparative perspective, the best available evidence leads us to conclude that the behavioral pattern we customarily refer to as love is a learned response conditioned in the individual in those societies where the pattern is rewarded, valued, and functional in the adaption of the individual to the institutionalized arrangements of his (or her) society, and in the maintenance of its institutions.

To use "love" as a scientific concept may be self-defeating and unproductive. The word has been and is used in a multitude of different ways as exemplified by such phrases as mother love, love of sports, loving one's country, loving people, or horses, or tomatoes, the stars on a clear night, the theater, etc. In these multiple senses, love might very well be considered universal. However, any concept that can mean just about anything to anyone is of little use in science. In this paper, therefore, I will use love to refer to a relationship which may be observed and which includes the following: 1) patterned, repetitive (for the same individual and for categories of individuals), and normative behavior; 2) specifiable attitudes; and 3) emotional states between persons of the opposite sex or on occasion of the same sex. This actually or potentially includes sexual activity.

In these pages I shall focus on love in the contemporary middle-class United States. As the late Clyde Kluckhohn (1949) indicated some time ago, one of the more important contributions of anthropology (with its comparative, cross-cultural perspective and intensive research in alien cultures and traditions) is that it enables us to see ourselves, the way we behave, and our customs and social institutions in perspective—not as absolute, "natural," and universal, but rather as sometimes unique, learned patterns that are the products of the development and evolution of our own cultural heritage. The work of anthropologists like Margaret Mead (1963) on sex and repression and the late Melville J. Herskovits (1941) and others on racial classification, culture, and prejudice are only two examples of the application of the insights from comparative anthropology to problems of our own culture.

The anthropologist viewing love in American society would tend to see it as a very important behavioral pattern. After describing it, he would examine it within its larger socio-cultural setting to see how it relates to other aspects of the culture and other institutions. Elsewhere I have attempted this in an effort to analyze love with respect to its functions and the contribution it makes to the working of American society (Greenfield, 1965).

In brief, I argued that contemporary America, as has so often been noted by others, is a highly materialistic society that places exceptionally high value on material things, i.e., goods and services. A case could be made for claiming that our shared definition of what is good and to be desired by individuals who constitute the society may be measured in commodities or things. Our standards of success, worth, prestige, and dignity are, for the most part, material standards. *Things* are important to us and much of our social life is spent in producing and accumulating these valued material objects.

Our material values, which are learned in the socialization process at an early age, provide us with a set of shared motives and goals for individual aspiration. If it is "natural" to want material possessions, which is to say that implicitly everyone agrees they are to be desired, then everyone—at least the vast majority—will strive to accumulate them. Indeed, much of our social structure consists of the detailed ways in which individuals may strive to acquire and accumulate the material items they tend to value so highly.

With respect to the process dimension of the total social system, to a very considerable degree the rewards offered to motivate individuals to occupy and perform most social roles provide access, either directly or indirectly, to material goods and services. The social machinery by means of which this

41

works is the market system and the role money plays within it. In short, money has come to serve as a substitute for the valued material goods and services since it can be converted at just about any time into commodities on the market. Hence, money, which equals things—given the market mechanism—can serve as a common standard representing a diversity of specific goods and services, thus taking into account individual preferences.

The valued material commodities are produced in the industrial-occupational sector of the social system. The relevant units or groups here are companies, firms, factories, etc.—social groups based on the bureaucratic model of social organization. Individuals are recruited to take job roles, and when they do and perform in conjunction with machines and other aspects of our industrial technology, the result is additional goods and/or services which then are placed on the market to be sold at a profit for the producing company or firm—its *raison d'etre*.

In the perceptions of most Americans, the occupational sector is perhaps the most important of our social institutions. Here can be found the means by which success is obtained and human social worth is defined.

The rewards offered to motivate individuals to occupy and perform roles in the occupational sector are material. It must be remembered that if individuals with the necessary training and skills were not recruited satisfactorily to occupy the positions or jobs in our occupational sector, the valued goods and services either would not be produced or would be produced in lesser quantities. Money in varying amounts is offered in the form of wages and salaries which can be converted through the market into commodities. Individuals trained to compete with each other offer themselves in an effort to acquire as much money, and hence things, as possible.

A case could be made for arguing that most of the roles in other sectors of American society also are filled by means of offering material, primarily monetary, rewards. Religious leaders, for example, are paid salaries and most churches are run on the model of businesses. The same is true in social, intellectual, and other areas. Even artists, poets, and musicians have been "professionalized" as part of the process of incorporating aesthetic activities into the general mold.

Many roles, however, such as memberships in the Eagles Club, the Republican Party, etc., do not provide salaries or other remuneration directly. Generally they are either filled by those already successful in the competition for jobs, incomes, and things, for the purpose of additional prestige; or they may be viewed as stepping-stones to make the contacts that provide potential deferred payoffs in jobs and increased incomes. In sum, most roles in the system are filled directly or indirectly by means of monetary or other material rewards.

Work and the rewards it brings to the individual are, therefore, highly valued in American society. Not all Americans work, however. Children, many women, and others generally classified as "dependents," who receive a share of the valued goods and services, must be articulated to the job-money-market system.

In addition to the company or firm—used generically to refer to all businesses, government agencies, churches, etc.—the second major structural unit or group in the American social system is the family, by which is meant a nuclear family household. It is this household unit, when articulated with the occupational sector through a wage-earner who holds a position in both a family and a firm simultaneously, that is critical in the distributive process of the economy and the society (Parsons and Bales, 1955).

The role obligations of the nuclear family household, among other things, require the one adult male to support his mate and their offspring. He does this by holding a job in the occupational sector and using the income earned to purchase material items to be consumed by himself and the remainder of the group, who are referred to as his "dependents." His mate, the only adult female in the group, is expected to give birth to, care for, and, in part, socialize the children; care for the residence (generally provided from the income he earns); cook meals, clean, etc. In addition, a major responsibility is for her to shop in the market for commodities to satisfy the basic and conditioned needs of her mate, herself, and their children with the money earned and provided by her mate—the specific definition of "to support."

From the perspective of the system, it is the shopping behavior of females in the numerous

44

households, made possible by the employment of their breadwinner-mates, that results in the clearing of the market and the distribution of the goods and services produced in the industrial-occupational sector to the population. The nuclear family household, in this way, plays a critical role in the distribution of the valued material goods and services.

The nuclear family is composed of a minimum of three social positions: 1) adult male, referred to as husband-father; 2) adult female, referred to as wife-mother; and 3) children, the biological or adopted offspring of the two adults, who are separated by sex and called son and daughter. The basis of the group is the conjugal relationship between the two adults.

The nuclear family household, as we have seen, plays a very important role in the workings of this materially-oriented society. Domestic groups, however, come into being new in each generation as the result of the voluntary decision of two adults to establish a socially sanctioned potential mating relationship.

The society in general values the acquisition and accumulation of material commodities. Roles within the domestic group, however, and particularly that of the husband-father which is the critical link between the productive sector and the units of consumption, require the role occupant to give away a considerable part of the money and the potential in goods and services it represents to other persons—a strange, i.e., unrelated and not previously known female and the children to whom she gives birth. Given the dominant values of the society, the ques-

45

tion legitimately may be asked: Why should young males, conditioned to work and strive for material accumulation, ever voluntarily choose to occupy a role (husband-father) whose primary activity is to give away that which is so highly valued and for which he has worked so hard to acquire? Why should men in this society ever voluntarily marry? In the terminology of classical economics, marriage may be viewed as a form of "irrational" behavior.

The answer to the question, as all participants in the culture know, is love. Men in American society and, in more and more cases, women also—in the name of love—sacrifice what from one perspective might be considered their socially defined personal best interests and assume the obligation of giving their valued and worked for material possessions for the support of others because they "love" them.

It is well known that the attitudes and sentiments of love are the antithesis of the ordinary material values of American society. Poets, novelists, playwrights, film and television writers, etc., regularly juxtapose the two sets of values, the one aimed at material accumulation by means of competition and the other focusing on giving, sharing, and cooperative concern for the dramatic effect produced. The hard-working hero struggles to achieve and accumulate materially with little concern for others until he is smitten by love. Then his entire countenance changes; his attitudes and behavior shift 180 degrees. When in love he cares for those he ignored, and perhaps even abused, previously. He no longer sees work and material acquisition as the end all.

Something more has been added to his life—something that enables him to transcend the ordinary and strive for "higher" rewards.

From the perspective of the dominant material values, the following may well be viewed as irrational choices of action: mating, marriage, and the establishment of nuclear households, and their associated obligations and responsibilities. On the other hand, if individuals of the opposite sex did not pair off, mate, and found new and independent domestic units that become consumers in the marketplace, amongst other things, the goods and services produced in the industrial-occupational sector would not be distributed. Profits would not be made by the producers and the larger economic system would begin to sputter and grind to a halt. Consequently, from the perspective of the larger social system, it may be considered necessary, for the continued working of the larger social system, for individuals, at some point in their life cycle, to behave irrationally and fall in love.

Love then, and the attitudes, sentiments, and behaviors associated with it, may be viewed as part of an alternative value system generating behaviors that integrate and make workable the larger social system. In one sense, the attitudes, sentiments, and behaviors associated with love may be viewed as incompatible with material values and behaviors. And, when not juxtaposed to produce the seeming dramatic opposition, but rather viewed along the trajectory of the life cycle the individual, love becomes a built-in and socially accepted excuse for temporary irrationality. Individuals in love can

47

"throw caution"—and almost everything else they have learned as part of their materialistic, competitive upbringing—"to the winds" and behave irrationally and not only be excused but reinforced and rewarded by their fellows. The shared expectation, which with great statistical regularity follows behaviorally, is that after a while they will "settle down" in conjugal domesticity and return to the struggle for material accumulation. They will get back to work, decorate, buy things for themselves and their home, have children and, in the name of love, behave rationally like everyone else once more.

Love, in middle-class American society, then, is a behavioral syndrome with repetitive and patterned behaviors, attitudes, and emotional states that is learned and rewarded and which makes possible the formation of the nuclear family households so vital to the total working of the socio-economic system. In brief, it represents the distinctive means, developed in the western world and associated with the reordering of society after the industrial revolution, to establish in each generation the numerous nuclear family domestic groups that complement and integrate the industrial-occupational-market system in the structuring of the total socio-cultural system.

It is interesting to note that the traditional prohibitions with respect to sex in the romantic love complex, in which sexual activity is to be deferred until and condoned only after and within a marriage, are breaking down. In the past and to a lesser degree today, sex was one, if not the primary, reward

48

(value) to be gained from marriage. Today, sex is in the process of being separated from marriage and a greater percentage of the population is participating in pre, post, extra, and nonmarital sexual activity. As significant as this change might appear to be at first glance, it is interesting to note that, from the perspective of the social structure, the new, emancipated love-sex arrangements still, for the most part, result in the formation of new nuclear households in which at least one of the members takes a job and works to provide support for the group.

At best guess, the future might have in store a reordering of middle-class American attitudes and values with respect to love, sex, and marriage. However, at least in the eyes of this observer, the innovations appear to be fully consistent with the continued performance of the traditional functions of the romantic love syndrome. And as long as individuals continue to behave in conflict with their material interests and to found new households that are supported through the job system and function as consumer units in the market, the total social system will be affected only minimally. The frosting, so to speak, might be changed, yielding something new on the individual level, but for the social system as a whole, the consequences appear most probably to be of only minor significance.

By way of conclusion, I should like to suggest for those of the persuasion to change American society that the logical implication of this argument is the following: in order to bring about significant social change, what is needed is not more love, but less, and perhaps none. If, as I have argued, love is a key element in the maintenance and continuity of the total social system, more love would only strengthen that system by producing more domestic units of consumers that will be articulated with the market through the job mechanism. In spite of the apparent surface changes and greater freedoms, i.e., breaking traditional sex taboos, marriage regulations, etc., the assumed oppressive system would be reinforced, not weakened. With the proposed decrease and possible elimination of love as a valued and rewarded pattern, however, the total social system would have to be reordered because it could not continue to function.

And for those who argue for more love, using the word in its most general sense, I can only say that what love appears to mean in this usage is something good as opposed to what exists, that is, our present set of social arrangements and patterned social relationships. It is these prevailing social arrangements that are viewed as bad and, therefore, to be changed. It is argued, for example, if we had more love for each other, for mankind, etc., that which is considered to be bad in human relationships would be improved. My response to this is: when what exists is found to be unsatisfactory, the constructive approach is to replace it with something more congenial. The replacement, however, must be something specific, i.e., behaviors and attitudes that may be described and analyzed, taught and learned. Asking for more love in the hope of something better without providing a blueprint for specific, patterned, situationally appropriate, and satisfying behaviors is really not very constructive. This is especially so in this case since love, the solution offered, already stands for a set of patterned, institutionalized behaviors that serve to maintain and support the very social system that is being criticized.

Finally then, I should have to side with Casler and say that on the socio-cultural level, as on the psychological, love may be like a crutch, impeding the development of new social forms so important for the development of a better and more satisfying human condition and society of the future.

REFERENCES

Greenfield, S. M. Love and marriage in modern America: A functional analysis. *The Sociological Quarterly*, 1965, Vol. 6, No. 4, pp. 361-377.

Herskovits, M. J. *The myth of the Negro past*. New York: Harper and Brothers, 1941.

Kluckhohn, C. *Mirror for man*. New York: Whittlesey House, 1949.

Mead, M. *Sex and temperament in three primitive societies*. New York: Morrow, 1963.

Parsons, T. and Bales, R. F. *Family, socialization and interaction process*. Glencoe, Illinois: The Free Press, 1955.

II. On the Critique of Romantic Love: Some Sociological Consequences of Proposed Alternatives

Sidney M. Greenfield

THE FOREGOING PAPER presents one hypothesis for explaining the existence of love in the contemporary United States and its prevalence, namely, that it constitutes a special reward-value system serving to induce and motivate otherwise not necessarily interested individuals to occupy the basic social positions in the domestic group of the society. I conclude the paper by arguing that many of those who are criticizing and rebelling against "the system" by attacking some of its elements in isolation-mating, courtship, and other patterned aspects of cross-sex interaction—are missing the boat, so to speak, focusing on the wagging tail rather than the dog. A more appropriate place to direct their criticism and apply their imagination and creative talents, I propose, is in changing the institutional system and its arrangements for producing and distributing goods and services and, more specifically, the material value premises that underlie the total system. With appropriate modifications in these areas, many of the behavioral patterns objected to by activists desirous of change would readily disappear, hopefully to be replaced by patterns more consistent with contemporary views of justice and equity. Much to my dismay, however, I see most of the efforts of social activists being directed towards criticizing and changing what sociologists might refer to as the dependent variable, the male-female relationships and the division of labor by sex and age within the domestic organization, but in such a way that the independent variable, the material values and social arrangements for the production and distribution of material goods and services, is reinforced. If my analysis is right, much of this effort is being misdirected. If greater social justice is the goal, alternative actions focused elsewhere might be considered to be in order.

As actors in society, we may debate whether or not love is a good or a bad thing. Personally, I have no standards other than my personal biases with which to judge. The comparative perspective of my discipline reveals that in some societies individuals readily fall in love and are rewarded, while in other societies persons exhibiting this behavioral pattern are subjected to reactions ranging from ridicule to physical harm. Between the extremes—high versus low incidence of the behavioral-attitudinal-emotional complex referred to as love—is a range of societies in which the pattern appears irregularly, with little

attention paid to the participants. Since no evidence
that I know of demonstrates a necessary positive
relationship between love and "happiness" or any
other social value, I can only conclude that love is
one of the many socio-cultural traits that is good for
social actors who define it as good, a priori, and not
necessarily good for those who do not define it in
that way. I conclude, therefore, that love, in its own
right, is not necessarily either good or bad but rather
that this depends upon the cultural context in which
the pattern is observed. This, of course, leads me to
say for the contemporary United States that there
is nothing, in its own right, necessarily wrong with
the criticism and ultimate rejection of love as a
value. The opposite, that love is good and to be
valued is as defensible—or indefensible—as the case
may be.

Speaking from the Olympian heights of an "objective" social science then, the placing of a positive
or a negative value on a behavioral pattern such as
love is up to the individuals who constitute the membership of a given society at a particular point in
time. Although limited by their prior socialization,
in theory and in fact, they are able to define and
redefine values as new consensuses are reached and
old ones redefined. As a member of a particular
society, I along with each of the others, may have
my opinion and preference—a preference I may be
willing to act on behalf of, and perhaps even argue,
fight, and become a martyr for—but this is
independent of my position as a scientist and a
scholar.

What I am saying is that as a social anthropologist I have no way of determining whether love is good or bad outside the context of the belief system shared by the members of a society. And when that belief system is in flux and in the process of being both challenged and defended by diverse segments of the population, I can offer little to adjudicate the dispute. However, what I can do, with the aid of the conceptual tools of social systems analysis, is to point up some of the possible consequences that might follow from the questioning and possible modification or elimination of once positively valued cultural patterns such as love. In addition, I can raise questions about suggested alternatives to specific patterns in terms of their ability to do specific tasks that may be: 1) requisites for other related institutional arrangements within the original system, or 2) requirements for continuity and survival of the society. If love as a cultural pattern makes a contribution to the maintenance and continuity of the larger American social system, its modification and/or elimination will create a void that must be filled in other ways. This, of course, does not preclude the possibility of combining a change in one part of a social system with changes in other areas that would permit maintenance and continuity of the total system. Scientifically this is neither good nor bad in its own right, but instead these evaluations depend upon the definitions of the members of the society engaged in the dynamic of modification, redefinition, and social change.

Although social science cannot provide standards

for judging and evaluating specific cultural patterns and social arrangements, it can make certain kinds of judgments in the broadest sense. If we view culture and social systems as adaptive mechanisms (as most sociologists and social anthropologists do), minimally we can view as "good" those arrangements that permit the continuity of the group across the generations and as "bad" those that are not successful in this respect. Regarding social and cultural behavior, we have learned that there is a series of requirements that must be satisfied by any human population if it is to survive. What the social scientist can do then, with respect to a discussion of social change, is to construct models to see whether or not proposed modifications in existing socio-cultural arrangements are compatible with survival requirements.

We can look at proposed challenges to love first in terms of the larger social system in which it is enmeshed. As indicated above, one significant contribution love makes at present to the maintenance and continuity of the larger social system of the United States is that it provides the motivation needed for individual adults to voluntarily occupy basic positions in the domestic group and perform expected roles. Each new generation "falls in love," pairs off, and establishes households independent of those of parents, relatives, and others. Consequently new units of consumption are created to absorb the ever increasing variety and quantity of goods and services being produced. And since there are no alternative sources of support available other than the job-wage-market combination, survival dictates that at least one member of the pair will enter the competition for an occupational position. This role, in addition to providing the income with which to purchase the goods and services for the domestic group to consume, forms part of one of the many social groups (i.e., firms, companies, etc.) that, as the result of the labor input of their many employees combined with capital and raw materials, produces the goods and services available in the market.

Love, however, also provides the primary motivation for mating—as opposed to nonprocreative sex —and the conception and birth of children. Children in American society are assumed to be born into a domestic group that is expected to take responsibility for their care and future socialization. (The orphan home or other institutionalized arrangements are exceptions to ensure the survival of the statistically small number of cases in which there is no domestic group to assume responsibility for a child.) There are only two adults in each nuclear family household, and one must be physically out of the household for some eight to ten hours per day at least to earn the income that is both the basis of subsistence and the measure of prestige, worth, and success for the group. This leaves only one person to perform the activities associated with: 1) socialization and child care, 2) the likewise critical job of purchasing the goods and services defined as "needed to live on," 3) caring for the children, and 4) showing to the world sufficient achievement in the quest for the accumulation of material valuables. Since there are only two adults in each domestic group, there is not much room for flexibility in the division and assignment of activities. Division of labor by age, or kinship, for example, or for that matter almost any other standard, is not possible. A simple division of labor by sex is the only option, and what we find as the general rule is males working at jobs outside the household and females caring for children and purchasing and maintaining material items that fill and are consumed within the household.

Consistent with the dominant material values of the society, far greater prestige and recognition is given to wage earning (especially to those successful at it since it brings with it the ability to obtain the material valuables that to some are a measure of worth and dignity) than to child rearing and the mere purchasing and care of goods and services. Hence, in increasing numbers in recent years, women (especially those who have been successful in climbing the rungs of the qualifying ladder of the school which both trains for and certifies admission into the competition for the more rewarding jobs) have combined work in the occupational sector, which enables them to compete for the material rewards of the society as individuals and not as a member of a pair, with the performance of other tasks. It should be mentioned that, at the lower end of the stratification ladder, women have been working, as well as bearing and caring for children and managing a household for many generations, but primarily in order to obtain the minimum income needed for survival of their domestic group. However, partly due to the expansion of opportunities for higher education today, more and more women are striving to enter the labor force to seek fulfillment and reward according to the traditional rules and standards of the larger society.

In the traditional division of labor by sex within the domestic group then, males have been assigned—and socialized for—those activities outside the household that are believed to be important and rewarding. Women, by contrast, have been assigned—but *not* necessarily socialized for—those activities that according to the values of the society are not very important and rewarding, and increasingly are being viewed as a degrading form of drudgery by some segments of the population.

Criticism of and elimination of the love syndrome would make vulnerable the domestic group as it is found at present. If not for love, what other reason would there be for individuals to pair off in mating relationships and establish separate households?

With respect to the system of producing and distributing the valued goods and services, if new households were not created to purchase and consume the commodities placed on the market, the system could no longer function. Likewise, from the perspective of the individual members of the society, in the absence of traditional family units and their role in distribution, how would they acquire the items needed and/or desired for their survival and prestige? One system being proposed by some self-styled radicals is for all adults to enter the labor force and earn income for their own subsistence and status placement.

This option could very well be satisfying to critical males who see the present love, mating, and household formation pattern as saddling them with "responsibilities" for spouses and offspring that are competitive with their efforts at material accumulation. It also could be satisfying to females who feel exploited by being assigned those tasks within the household that are not regarded as socially valuable. Furthermore, it would free them from what may be viewed as dependency upon a male who currently is expected to provide them with material commodities.

As it appears now, this possibility would make every adult a wage earner and responsible for his or her own support. One expectation might be that each adult then would become a unit of consumption in the market comparable to an existing household; this would increase significantly the number of consumers competing for products in the market. Needless to say, if each adult were to have his or her own apartment and appropriate furnishings, etc., this would be a significant structural change that would stimulate business and make happy the heads of the firms that dominate the economy.

One consequence of this hypothesized system in which all adults are to become wage earners is that the economy, as presently constituted, cannot possibly absorb the increasing numbers who will be looking for work. In fact, as is generally well known, the American economy, due to automation and other factors, is scarcely able to absorb the male household heads currently seeking employment in order to support mates and children in the current system. Moreover, with modern technology it is possible to produce more goods and services with less labor. Therefore, industry can handle an expanding market but it really has little need for an increase in the number of wage earners. Under the present system, unemployment and underemployment is a problem that is expected to increase in the future. The redefinition of all adults as potential wage earners might very well create a situation in which perhaps as much as half the population will be unable to find employment. And, it must be remembered, independent wage earners in a market system who are without income are unable to obtain even minimum subsistence. Close to half of the population might have to be provided for if the larger system is to survive.

One condition that could make this proposed system more likely is for jobs to be reduced from 8 hours per day and 40 hours per week to perhaps 2 or 3 hours per day and perhaps 10 or 12 hours per week. The question, however, would be whether industry, as it is presently constituted, could pay the wages demanded by laborers and their unions for the shorter working periods.

Let us assume, however, that such an economic reordering is possible. This still leaves open the question of noneconomic social arrangements. If each individual is to be an independent wage earner, what social groupings would he belong to other than those associated with his work, occupation, or profession?

I raise this question because it is related to another area that love, in theory at least, is expected to provide answers for in American society. I refer to the broad area of patterned, interpersonal relations and social bonds of closeness and intimacy. As is generally known, social relations in the world of industry and work are mostly of the variety referred to by sociologists as secondary relationships. That is, they are impersonal and focus on very specific and clearly delimited transactions. Primary relationships in American society are mostly those of the family and friendship, with the love-mating pattern supposedly the basis for the closest and most intense relationship of all.

Loneliness, isolation, and alienation are currently considered to be among the more important social-psychological problems present in our society. Social change in the direction of all adults becoming wage earners, paralleled with a de-emphasis on love, I submit, would intensify loneliness, isolation, and feelings of alienation. I see little to be gained by this, and I suggest that some thought be given to the question of new soical groupings that emphasize affective, warm social relationships and to the means by which individuals will be recruited for membership and participation in such groups and relationships. I suggest in thinking about this problem that care be taken to remove from the individual the burden of establishing such relationships. It may well turn out, after more detailed examination and analysis, that the basis for much of the isolation, loneliness, and alienation in traditional urban-industrial American society is the absence of institutional patterns for membership, participation, and behavior in groups. As it is now, the individual must sink or swim, so to speak, on his or her own in adjusting and relating to other persons and groups. There is little in the way of tradition and cultural pattern to assist him. As a result, each individual, amongst other things, is left fraught with anxiety that might be reduced considerably if institutionalized arrangements were established that assumed some of the responsibility which currently rests solely on the shoulders of the individual.

Perhaps much of the contemporary problem of American domestic organization—broken and unhappy homes, disenchantment and rebellion against the love ideal, etc.—is related to the fact that each individual customarily is expected to work out for himself relationships in those areas that emphasize affection, care, and intimacy. The problem with "love" and with the American mating and domestic system may well be that too much is expected of an individual who is not aided by social norms and cultural traditions. Change in the direction of greater individualization might well intensify the problem rather than help it.

By way of conclusion, I should like to descend from the Olympian heights to which I retreated earlier. I do this to express a personal fear as to the direction in which I see many activists and radicals moving. I too may be critical of the romantic love syndrome. However, in contrast with numerous others, I see love as a cultural pattern that is related to other aspects of the American social system; and it is to the broader system, of which love is a functional and integral part, that I think the real effort at reform and change should be directed. I refer specifically to the material values that underpin our American way of life and to the existing institutional arrangements for the distribution of the valued goods and services.

As I listen to various radicals and reformers, I have the impression that the changes they advocate will in the long run reinforce and perhaps even reinvigorate the present socio-cultural system. For example, some persons see greater individualization and increased participation in the industrial, job-wage system as "liberation" from the deficiencies of the present love-mating-family system. But this seems to be reaffirming what I, for one, consider to be the worst in the American tradition, that is, our tendency to define human worth, dignity, and fulfillment in terms of occupational and professional achievement.

65

I can understand that as things are at present, American women may be, for the most part, relegated to the performance of activities that are not given the major rewards of the society. The problem, as I see it, however, is in those values and the reward system itself and not in the access of women or other categories and groups to this system.

Defining human worth and dignity in terms of successful competition for jobs, salaries, occupational positions, and their associated material rewards is to me an anathema that degrades all sectors of the society. Although some may consider this next point as male chauvinism, I happen to think American women are lucky, and not deprived, because the vast majority do not have to enter the competitive struggle for jobs, promotions, and salaries that have brought to their male counterparts ulcers, heart conditions, and an average life span some five years shorter than theirs. That intelligent women interested in social change as a means of improving the human condition should want this, leaves me in utter confusion. As a male, I for one wish that I did not have to work so that I could do the many things that to me would be more rewarding, but this would make me subject to criticism and sanction in the society in which I live.

As members of society and as fellow human beings, I hope we can press together for changes that would liberate us all—male and female, young and old, black and white—from the chains of competition in an impersonal world of jobs, wages, and possessions with their associated bases in stratification and separation. Reforms supporting and reinforcing the values that define human worth and dignity in terms of work and the present occupational system, even where these reforms give access to rewards to those presently denied such access, I can do without. They are at best transitory, and only postpone the task of basic reform that is so badly needed.

In socio-cultural terms then, love may be criticized; but if the root problems of the society are to be dealt with, more than the surface manifestations and criticisms must be considered. Alternatives to love, mating, and the domestic organization of American society must be consistent with a new order of social values and institutions and not, albeit inadvertently so, with modifications that most probably will strengthen the existing material values and social arrangements.

3

I. The Case for Love

Louis J. Karmel

THE PROBLEM IN discussing love is, of course, its nebulous nature. It is even more difficult to discuss when one brings scientific knowledge and approaches to bear on this four letter word. Attempts to apply the rigorous standards and language of science to its definitions can end in utter futility by cleansing the concept of all its meanings. Other areas have been so treated in the application of scientific procedures to human behavior. On the other hand, if one invokes sentimentality and poetic license he will be discredited as a scientist in the same way that the writer-poet would be if he interlaced his poetry and prose with scientific verbiage.

Another problem besetting an objective discussion of love is that the term is fraught with so many different meanings—from a mystical state of communication to a sexual liaison or a general "good" feeling.

Freud (1959), in his investigations in the development of the sexual life of the human organism, first brought scientific methodology to bear upon the whole subject of love. His basic thesis was that one does not "fall" in love but grows into love; love grows within the individual. According to Freud, this process starts in infancy (Menninger, 1942). The infant, utilizing all the organs of his body, attaches himself to a series of love objects, for example, his parents, siblings, and later his peers and adult companions. The major objective of this paper is to define what is meant by love and to present its antagonistic counterpart, hate. I make the basic assumption of an admixture of two drives, one erotic and the other destructive, residing in the human organism. This is based, of course, on Freud's theory of Eros and Thanatos. Thus, a psychoanalytic point of view permeates (although without excluding other perspectives) the basic philosophical underpinnings of my approach to love.

As a definition of love, let us take Fenichel's (1945) statement: "One can speak of love only when consideration of the object goes so far that one's own satisfaction is impossible without satisfying the object, too [p. 84]." Fenichel (1945) credits Fromm with stating:

> "Persons in whom the genital primacy is lacking, that is orgastically impotent persons, are also incapable of love. The full capacity for love not only changes the relations towards other persons but also the

relation toward one's own ego. The contrast between object love and self-love again is a relative one: in primary narcissism there is self-love instead of object love; in secondary narcissism there is a need for self-love (self-esteem) which overshadows object love. With the capacity for object love another, higher, post narcissistic type of self respect becomes available. [p. 85]."

Thus, at the height of full genital satisfaction, a personal identification comes back on a higher level that is a feeling of togetherness, of loss of individuality, and of achieving an appropriate reunion of the ego with something larger which has been beyond the pale of the individual ego (Fenichel, 1945). In essence then, this writer sees love as a basic instinct. It is one of the two basic instincts of man, namely Eros, the life instinct. (The other basic instinct is Thanatos, the death instinct, the aggressive instinct of man.) Repression of one causes pathology rather than the overt expression or channelization of the other. Fenichel (1945) states, "In a normal, genitally oriented person aggressiveness is a means of achieving his goals under certain adverse circumstances; the repression of these means may create as much a handicap in life as the repression of the ability to love [p. 86]." Love is not a learned emotion but an innate quality of the human condition. Remember that these two instinctual impulses are an admixture within each individual and are mixed in various proportions according to the unique personality. It should be remembered, therefore, that this presupposes that there is no such thing as pure love or pure hate. Thus, love is not pathological per se any more than hate is pathological since their uniqueness is a matter of degree and both are indigenous to the human organism.

Casler (1969) views love as pathological. He makes the point that society emphasizes the need for love to precede sex, e.g., "The mores of our society discourage us from seeking sexual gratification from anyone with whom we do not have a preexisting relationship [p. 18]." I am afraid that Dr. Casler is referring to a previous society. The trend today is not for loving as much as for sexing. Nevertheless, it is necessary to look further and examine the idea that we love because of social convention and not because of basic ego needs. I contend that we love not because of social convention itself but because of our own intrinsic needs to relate to others and away from our own narcissistic component. The person who cannot love is usually fixated on a pregenital level of development. That is, his gratification takes an inward object. The genital person, on the other hand, is an adult who loves another human. The pregenital person is still primarily concerned with his own narcissistic feelings.

Love is not caused by the need for security, sex, or social conformity although these may be components of love. People sometimes engage in dependency without love, e.g., in hate relationships: dependence on mother-security keeps the son with her but does not produce love; on the contrary it produces hate. Sex is engaged in by thousands without any hint of love. People who pick mates from different ethnic, religious, social, and economic strata are usually not conforming to social pressures; rather, they have deviated from the accepted norm. Thus, it is hard to see how these could be seen as conforming to society.

Casler goes on to state, "Nothing is good or bad but culture makes it so [p. 20]." This is a simplistic view because the taboos against certain practices, such as murder of one's own blood and/or tribal peers, are almost universally accepted as a violation of cultural mores. Further, to say that nothing is good or bad but what culture makes it is to say that man has no control over his unique destiny and is completely a puppet of the culture in which he is cultivated.

It is very difficult to study love in a laboratory because of the mystical quality of love and the difficulty in defining what love is. Casler states that in the laboratory ". . . . no physiological indices have been discovered for love [p. 20]." This is absurd when the very word is a hypothetical construct which gains its relevancy by definition. It exists no more than "mind" or "soul" for scientific purposes unless given or postulated. Therefore, how could it be quantitatively measured in the laboratory?

The scientist or logical positivist who expects to unlock the doors to the mystery of life in the laboratory has as fantastic a faith in science as his ancestors had in religion. The scientist who attempts to interject love into a laboratory setting is by the very nature of the proposition dehumanizing the state we call love. For example, Casler (1969) states, "Recent experiments suggest a relationship between the skin and pleasure centers in the brain. Should this research continue to be fruitful, we will have an explanation of love in terms of the workings of the central nervous system [p. 20]." To make such an explanation is to have decided beforehand that authorities agree upon what love is because in order to measure a given condition in a scientific setting one must have certain definitions. Since love is so nebulous, it seems ludicrous to state that it can be measured in a laboratory under laboratory conditions.

Why must the scientist perseverate on the idea that love must foster anything but love? The scientist who claims that people in love are more mature is just as much in error as the scientist who claims that to love is pathological. The moment of being loved and loving is the important reality, not maturity or any other stated consequences. It is easy for the scientist to label people as insecure or as secure. It is easy for people to say that the person in love is insecure and therefore needs to find a mate who provides security. However, it can be stated with a large measure of certitude that there are no secure people in the universe. Who can be the secure person? All men are by necessity of being, i.e., of living, insecure. This is because no man is secure or sure of everlasting physical life. On the contrary, he knows his life is temporary and tenuous and subject to conditions that are completely beyond his control. All men suffer from existential anxiety, be it conscious or unconscious.

It is this writer's contention that to be unable to love is pathological because it reveals an inability of the organism to join forces or relate to another being, in other words, a fixation at the narcissistic level of development.

Love is not based entirely on insecurity, conformity, or sex. It is based on the human need or instinct, if you will, to complete the gestalt of humanism; that is, the circle of love is the joining of humans together. Man has developed communities because of his need to complete the circle. Without his fellow being he is incomplete. The love-free person is egotistical in the sense of being fixated at the narcissistic level of development. To love is to enjoy the fruits of the human condition; to love is to be an adult human being; to love is to the human as blooming is to the flower. Plato said, "For love is the desire of the whole, and the pursuit of the whole is called love." Many years later, the same theme was expounded when Jesus taught, "God is love"; while in recent times, the Eastern philosopher and teacher Meher Baba (1967) has stated, "Love is the most significant thing in life. . . . God is not understood in His essence until He is also understood as *infinite love* [pp. 173-175]."

REFERENCES

Baba, M. *Discourses by Meher Baba, Vol. III.* (6th ed.). San Francisco: Sufism Reoriented Inc., 1967.

Casler, L. This thing called love is pathological. *Psychology Today,* 1969, 18-76.

Fenichel, O. *The psychoanalytic theory of neurosis.* New York: W. W. Norton & Company, 1945.

Freud, S. *Collected papers, Vol. 4.* New York: Basic Books, Inc., 1959.

Menninger, K. *Love against hate.* New York: Harcourt, Brace & Co., 1942.

II. Love Is the Essence of Life

Louis J. Karmel

MY ESTEEMED COLLEAGUES, I bring you greetings from Eros, Kama, and Venus as they are reflected and exist in my being. The breath of life is ignited by the spark of love. To live without love is to die without living. In death there is no love but only the darkness of nothingness. The demise of life is the dissolution of love. To live is to love. To love is to be.

I weep and despair for you who have died and for those of you who are dying. I see the spark of love slowly flickering and with it the end of being. The cult of death, that is, the squeezing out of the human spirit, is gaining the upper hand. All about us we see the denial of love. This rejection takes many forms, from the acting-out leaders of nations and their followers who coldly plot the physical and psychological deaths of people to the highly intellectualized who pour water on the flame of life by denouncing its love nucleus as an "illness" or as a commodity while others even question its very existence.

To weep over this contemporary condition is not to be shocked or even surprised. All people have within them two basic instincts, Eros and Death. These two instinctual impulses operate in various proportions within each human being. Eros is composed of basic and diffuse sexual needs and artistic and creative drives while the Death instinct encompasses the drives of extinction, aggressivity, hostility, and other base behaviors of people. If within each of us there is an admixture of these instincts, we cannot posit pure love or pure hate within a living organism. To extend this thesis to its final conclusion, we may state that to live is to love and to die, but to die is to die. Therefore, in all of us, the admixture ceases at physical death and the final victor is always Death. As Shakespeare has so eloquently stated: "Golden lads and girls all must / As chimney sweepers come to dust."

Thus the tragedy of life is not its final resolution, for we have no choice but stoical acceptance of the grim reaper of time. The tragedy of life is the victory of death among the living.

If, in fact, love is the essence of life, what is love? This is a hard question to answer, because love is a nebulous concept that, moreover, is applied to many differing situations. Since the term love is so hard to define, shall we throw it out or place specific kinds of adjectives, which denote specific behaviors, in front of it, such as sexual love or parental love, to signify exactly what we mean? My answer is "no" to both alternatives, for in my definition all forms of love are a variation of the same theme or instinct.

78

My definition of love is the act of deriving personal satisfaction from giving pleasure to another living being.

If love is a state of satisfaction emanating from the pleasure of our beloved, can we be lustful, greedy, egocentric, or objective in loving? The answer, of course, is no. To love and be loved is, to quote Segal (1970), "not ever having to say you're sorry [p. 131]." This statement not only signifies acceptance of the inevitable physical demise of one or both parties but the possible life-death, i.e., termination of the love bond. In addition, Segal is presenting the apex of adult love, whose base starts with narcissistic involvement in one's own physical and emotional needs and graduates to the zenith of adulthood which is the satisfaction of deriving pleasure by giving to another human being.

Today in the heat of both real and imagined oppression, our contemporary climate avails itself more to the death instinct than its love counterpart. In breaking loose from the shackles of repression, General Death and his subordinates, Hate and Aggression, are taking the lead. Death and hate are being replaced by death and hate. In the name of freedom, foreign peoples are burned to death "for their own good." In the name of progress and revolution, domestic lives and property are lost. In the name of equality and freedom, people are taught to hate each other: blacks vs. whites, females vs. males. Where will it end? Truly, Death is among the living.

All of the Death pushers are not, however, so blatant. The subtle types wear clothes of objectivity and science. Their tragedy is both personal and universal. Personal because in most cases they do not know what they are doing. Universal because they seduce others to their "scientism." Their unconscious death wishes are cloaked with conscious and sincere dedication to reason and science. They do not realize that by attempting to quantify that ingredient of the human condition labeled love they are destroying it—because to look for love in physical measurements is to prevent one's feelings or impulses from erupting, i.e., it blocks one's *being*. The surest way to lose love is to reach for it. Love is a feeling state, not an act of cognition. Love is what one feels at a given moment in time. To analyze it is to destroy it.

To live is to love. To love in this sense is to take a chance. To live and to love is to gamble. Loving entails risks, such as not being loved. The measurement and quantification of sexual "love" may be for some people a defense used to ward off the love impulses which might endanger the ego and place the person in a precarious position. One's self-esteem can be endangered by loving. If, however, love is nothing more or less than a hypothetical construct which expresses chemical and electrical changes in the body, what is lost if a union is unsatisfactory or if one does not take place? Surely this has nothing to do with you as a person—it's all the fault of incompatible chemistry. How convenient not to have to risk our egos. How convenient for us that

80

the scientists have erected ready-made defenses of rationalization and displacement.

Is a physiological response enough to give meaning to life? Does the mother react to her child only in terms of functional and organic S-R bonds? Is the human being no different from his or her ancestral animal-legacy? Is the size of the cerebral cortex the only distinguishing feature between man and the lower animals?

Meher Baba (1967), a philosopher who attempted to bridge the eastern and western worlds, states:

"In the animal world love becomes more explicit in the form of *conscious impulses* which are directed toward different objects in the surroundings. . . .

Human love is much higher than lower forms of love because human beings have the fully developed form of consciousness [p. 157]."

Baba (1967), in discussing the dynamics of love, states that:

"It constitutes the entire significance of creation. If love is excluded from life, all the souls in the world assume complete externality to each other and the only possible relations and contacts in such a loveless world are superficial and mechanical.

It is because of love that the contacts and relations between individual souls become significant. It is love which gives meaning and value to all the happenings in the world . . . [p. 164]."

In the name of love grave wrongs have been inflicted on men and women. Love has been used as an excuse for "keeping people in their place." One example is the peasant who is told that God "loves" him and that in eternity he shall be rewarded. Other examples are the women as well as some men, who have been placed in psychological bondage by the Hollywood—True-Confession romantic love ideal. On the one hand exploitative social conditions are excused in the name of eternal love and, on the other hand, females have been indoctrinated with the so-called love ideal to the point of losing their individuality. Shall we throw out love because its ideal has been used to control people? More importantly, does this type of so-called love fit my definition of giving to another human? Using and manipulating people is not love. Do we throw out our heritage, both potential and actualized, because the term love has been misused while real love has atrophied?

Kierkegaard (1962) speaks directly to this point:

"one may make the mistake of calling love that which is really self-love: when one loudly protests that he cannot live without his beloved but will hear nothing about

love's task and demand, which is that he
deny himself and give up the self-love of
erotic love. Or a man may make the mistake of calling by the name of love that
which is weak indulgence, the mistake of
calling spoiled whimpering, or corrupting
attachments, or essential vanity, or selfish
associations, or flattery's bribery, or mo-
mentary appearances, or temporal relationships by the name of love [p. 25]."

The basic point is that an erroneous label placed on
certain observed behaviors does not necessarily
negate the validity of the label. A society's establishment will use all types of devices including the big
lie in order to preserve the status quo. To reject love
because it has been misrepresented is to reject all of
the nobler values of peoples because they have been
misused.

No Virginia, you don't have to love in order to
have an orgasm. Yes Virginia, reduction of
physiological needs is important. Yes Virginia, you
can have both sex and love, although love is not
necessary for sex. Love is, however, necessary for
life. To exist without loving is possible. To live without loving is impossible.

Buber (1958), in commenting upon love, differen-
tiates between love and accompanying feelings. He
states:

"Feelings accompany the metaphysical
and metapsychical fact of love, but they do

83

not constitute it. The accompanying feelings can be of greatly differing kinds. The
feeling of Jesus for the demoniac differs
from his feeling for the beloved disciple;
but the love is the one love. Feelings are
entertained: love comes to pass. Feelings
dwell in man; but man dwells in his love
[p. 14]."

To love is not to be dependent, insecure, or an
establishment type. To feel independent and secure
does not mean one loves. The life-love equation can
be stated neither in terms of sensory modalities nor
normal-abnormal parameters. As stated in my first
paper, "The moment of being loved and loving is
the important reality, not maturity or any other
stated consequences." But the inability to love is existence without being. It reveals a pathological condition because it isolates the person from human relationships. An existence with only "I" is only existence. And existence with "I" and "thou" is life. As
Buber (1958) states:

"Love is responsibility of an *I* for a *Thou*.
In this lies the likeness—impossible in any
feeling whatsoever—of all who love, from
the smallest to the greatest and from the
blessedly protected man, whose life is
rounded in that of a loved being, to him
who is all his life nailed to the cross of the
world, and who ventures to bring himself

to the dreadful point—to love *all men* [p. 15]."

The last ten to fifteen years have been years of change. Our attitudes towards race, sex, peace, and war have at the very least been modified and in some cases dramatically altered. In the midst of this change, our society has been left with few of the old guidelines. This has caused widespread moral chaos and alienation. We have gone through successive stages of being "beat," "involved" (both nonviolently and violently), "hippies," women's liberation, humanistic (as sometimes seen in encounter and T-groups), and structured (as seen in behavior modification approaches). What is it that our people want? What is it that you and I want?

I believe the answer is life, i.e., love. We all want love. The present "Jesus Freaks" movement is certainly a reflection of this basic human need. Our young people are tiring of sex and drugs as answers to life. They want more, they want love.

Love cannot be purchased in a drug. It cannot be secured by "M and M's." It cannot be obtained through hating those who oppose us. It cannot be gained by destroying others. It cannot be established by loving only those who agree and respect us.

Two thousand years ago Jesus said (The New English Bible, 1970):

"Love your enemies and pray for your persecutors. . . . If you love only those who

love you, what reward can you expect?
Surely the tax-gatherers do as much as
that. And if you greet only your brothers,
what is there extraordinary about that? [p.
8, Chapter 5, verses 44-47]."

It is imperative for those of us who can still love
to divest ourselves of the chains of hate. The final
hour is approaching. Shall we choose hate and
destruction, objectivity and emotional sterility; or
shall we choose life and love? Shall we take the
chance—yes, the gamble of being enslaved by our
concern for love or shall we play it safe and be cool
in the face of the alternative of human robots who
respond to predetermined stimuli?

What will your choice be? To hate and destroy
your brothers and sisters? To play it cool in robot
fashion? Or will you choose life and love? Will you
choose to love without conscious preconditions and
to give yourself to another human being? Truly, this
is man at his best.

REFERENCES

Baba, M. *Discourses by Meher Baba, Vol. I.* (6th ed.).
San Francisco: Sufism Reoriented Inc., 1967.

Buber, M. *I and thou* (2nd ed.). New York: Charles
Scribner's Sons, 1958.

Kierkegaard, S. *Works of love: Some Christian reflections
in the form of discourses.* New York: Harper &
Row, 1962.

Segal, E. *Love story*. New York: The New American Library, Inc., 1970.

The New English Bible. Cambridge, England: The Syndics of the Cambridge University Press, 1970.

4

Love Is Neither Necessary
Nor Sufficient

Rogers H. Wright

IN ASSERTING THAT love is neither necessary nor sufficient, I am specifically referring to an individual's functioning essentially as an adult. I do not think I would care to defend—and perhaps no one could defend—the idea that love, at least as it is manifested in suckling, stroking, etc., is an unimportant thing in the early life experience. Therefore, it is not my intent to rule love off the psychological track. Rather, I want to look at love from the standpoint of a practicing clinical psychologist.

To any therapist who works with people, it becomes rapidly apparent that this thing called "love" is strange and wondrous indeed. Casler, in his paper in this volume, highlights an old clinical truism, namely, that much of what is called love is indeed dependence upon an external person as a source of gratification for the individual's inner needs. Indeed, clinicians have long known and described the frequently-encountered person whose acceptance of self or self-love is altogether conditional on external acceptance of love. But I do not wish to deal with the varieties of love one encounters, clinically or otherwise. Rather, as psychotherapists, it seems to me that a look at our obsession with love is long overdue. While I could not fully support the idea that love is pathological, I can certainly agree that our preoccupation with it might be.

Casler notes that one criterion of maturity in practically any theory of personality is the "capacity for love." One need only note the myriad articles, symposia, etc., to conclude that, as a culture, "we have love on the brain." In many instances, the explicit goal of a psychotherapeutic relationship is to make a person "more loving." I call to your attention, however, that the key word in the aforenoted definition of maturity is *capacity* for love, not necessarily that one actuates or utilizes that capacity. I, personally, would like to suggest another area that seems to me worthy of consideration. As I have viewed, both clinically and theoretically, our preoccupation with love, I am impressed more and more with the fact that perhaps, as psychologists, we really never left our basic roots in religion and philosophy. A basic tenet of most religious and/or philosophic systems is that aggression is "bad." Strikingly enough, whereas we can find an unlimited number of therapists who would take the position that love is good, I wonder how many psychologists we could find who would take the position that aggression is good. Certainly, we speak of it and support the people we see, at times, in experimenting with some aggressive actions, but this is, by the very nature of our work, dealing with people in trouble. How much, if any, of our psychologizing or theorizing or philosophizing really takes into account the possibility that aggression may serve an extremely useful purpose in the development of the child.

As I view the current social scene, I am impressed with the bumper stickers, etc., which lambaste us visually and aurally with the thesis "peace is good," "make love, not war," etc. I have come to wonder if perhaps in our preoccupation with love we are not really covering up and trying to deny some basic discomfort with hostility and aggression. I think one might make a case for this sociologically and, in fact, in reviewing material for this symposium, I reread Robert Ardrey's *The Territorial Imperative* (1966) and Desmond Morris' *The Naked Ape* (1967). In speaking of the importance of territory, Robert Ardrey makes the point "He who has will probably hold." It is a law that rings harshly to the contemporary ear, but this is a defect of the ear, not the law. In the territorial species, "[territory] has been the source of all freedom, the curse on the despot and the last desperate roadblock in the path of the aggressor's might." Audrey not too subtly suggests that one important aspect of loving is that a family, which usually derives therefrom, makes it numerically more probable that one will hold the territory to which one is attached.

As intellectuals we are steeped in Judeo-Christian

philosophy and ethics and confronted with our own hangups relating to passivity and our obsessions and needs for vicarious participation in lives we could not possibly live. Therefore, I wonder specifically if we, as psychotherapists, have not attempted to gloss over things that make us most uncomfortable because we have neither the philosophic rationale nor the personal inclination to deal with such feelings. Is it not possible that our admonitions to love (since it is essentially a passive proclivity) might be a defense against an active and/or aggressive approach to our world? Or may it not be a defense against our own lack of masculinity and/or femininity?

As, hopefully, a reasonably honest man and therapist, I have viewed with considerable interest the development of nude marathons, nude encounter groups, etc. Some of the points raised by the people involved in these activities do strike a chord that one must think about, for example, "getting down to the guts of it," "the defensive use of our clothing," etc. I have struggled with this issue for some time and have finally resolved it in my own mind, not by discounting altogether as exhibitionism the preoccupation with nudity, closeness, touching, feeling, etc., but rather with the idea that this is not love at all. From what I have observed clinically of patients I see who participate in such groups (completely aside from the obvious sexual hangups, etc.), there seems to be a basic noninvolvement on the part of these people which allows them to be nude and touching, ostensibly exchanging feelings, etc., while really remaining detached and aloof.

Basically, I think maybe we are just afraid of dealing with feelings that increasingly are going out of style. At least as I have viewed things, I can no longer accept as sine qua non for the definition of maturity "the capacity to love." I would have to broaden the definition to say that whereas one may need the capacity for love, one also needs to be comfortable with his hostility and aggression.

Thus, in closing, I really cannot buy Casler's ideas, at least where he goes so far as to suggest that love may impede the exercise of our own potential for growth and thus tend to perpetuate itself, because here it sounds much too much as if Casler is defining love in terms of the pathologic dependency that oftentimes masquerades as love. Either that, or it is suspiciously similar to the oftheard comment of the homosexual, designed to prove that homosexuality is a desirable state of affairs. I think the capacity for love, as well as the capacity for aggression, for philanthropy, for honesty, and even for intellectualizing may all be signs of maturity in a human being. We, as psychologists and intellectuals, are so damned glib in explaining ourselves and our motives that I think we are often philosophically the victims of the games we play.

I would like to see some shift away from our obsession with love into a more open area where we do not impose a hidden scale of values, no matter how implicit. I can certainly agree with Casler that one way of imposing conformity is, of course, the insistence on a concensually validated value system implicit in our psychological work.

REFERENCES

Ardrey, T. *The territorial imperative*. New York: Atheneum, 1966.

Morris, D. *The naked ape*. New York: McGraw-Hill, 1967.

5

Perspectives of a
Feminist Therapist

Annette M. Brodsky

"EVEN AS LOVE crowns you so shall he crucify you. Even as he is for your growth so is he for your pruning . . . " (Gibran, 1923). Love, as it is popularly conceived today, has a significantly restrictive social-cultural component which is used to encourage individuals to accept and perpetuate values that they do not want and that are not necessary for their well-being. Much of what passes for mature love is functionally obsolete. People in our society who are at an age and circumstance where they are considering commitments to long-term intimate relationships are in many cases thoroughly confused by the romanticized, archaic notions of love that they read in marriage manuals, advice columns, and for that matter professional psychiatric and psychological literature.

Our mores and life styles seem to be changing faster than everything but the explanations for them. The college students I see as a therapist and teacher are presenting problems of intimacy and relationships that do not exist in our framework of traditional marriage and premarital behavior. Dating, engagements, marriages based on clear divisions of labor, and absolute sexual fidelity are not necessarily desired by some of these couples. As therapists we tend to see things from our own frame of reference, and as a feminist therapist, I have become aware of the irrational thinking that accompanies our expectations for men and women in love.

Some of the still current myths about love between men and women are naturally dying. But, thanks to professionals and quasiprofessionals who have authority and therefore influence on individual's behaviors, the death is often in the form of a slow torture. The patient is encouraged to fight against the societal current in a futile, drawn-out series of temporary adjustments with an unrealistic hope for a return to his original life situation. The myths that are apparent to me to be most in need of revision in the current zeitgeist include the following:

1. Only a mature person can have a good love relationship, or, to be in love is synonymous with being a mature adult.

2. When two people are in love they become as one (whither thou goest, I will go).

3. A woman lives for love; for a man it is only one part of his life.

4. Lovers are selfless, concerned more about their loved ones than themselves.

5. Separate roles and functions that polarize the sexes are necessary for erotic love.
6. Women want to be dominated; men want a woman to lean on them.

Society has always restricted mating patterns to maintain its continuance under pressure. Religious, racial, and social class restrictions have been prime obstacles to the pairing of couples based on romantic attractions as persons. Romeo and Juliet can be seen as a case of conflict between social pressure and personal motivation. While we idolize the depth of their commitment to each other and their unselfish, altruistic caring for each other, their love was extremely pathological in the sense of being maladaptive for their own survival. Relationships that become intense enough to forgo social restrictions can also be intense enough to ignore the other needs of the lovers.

Today, only women are likely to see their lives as revolving around love. Present-day Juliets are still taught to overlove. As for a present-day Romeo, wherefore art thou? He's laughed at, considered foolish. When women are raised to see their natural function in life as the selfless, devoted caretakers of their husbands and children, then we are indeed saying to them that to love is to be mature. Is it any wonder that women so glibly talk of falling in love or so desperately seek it that they are willing to pay the price of many other needs such as self-determination, approval of persons other than the love object, individual identity, vocational goals, independent striving for success, and all the other male-identified goals? Men are told that love of a mate is one of a number of important aspects of the good life; for a woman it *is* her life. As Lord Byron said, "Man's love is of man's life a thing apart, 'Tis a woman's whole existence." Edith DeRham (1965) has analyzed the exploitive implications of that myth: "Women are expected to concentrate their lives on men, who in turn, concentrate on work. Thus women become the victims of a kind of fraud in which their love is exploited and in which they are somehow persuaded that they are involved in a legitimate action . . . if women are to live by sentiment, that is, love, and men by action, or work, they are clearly operating on two different levels at all times, related to each other as parallels that can never meet." What women really want is to be able to have options more like men, "to have freedom from emotional pettiness, to balance dependency on human relationships with activities of the mind."

The politics of love may have served to keep American women happy in the place where society felt they belonged. However, one of the consequences of the disenchantment with the feminine mystique and, later, the women's rights movement, has been to awaken the awareness of women to their discontent regarding their relationships with men and their position in the structure of society. They realize that they have been sold the position of homemaker in the name of love and for them love and altruism have become fused. The task force on

98

Family Law and Policy (1968) concluded that American women lose ground in personal development and self-esteem during the years of their married life. People become what they do. A married woman may see herself as wife, mother, and housekeeper, but in actuality she spends more time as housekeeper than in either of the other roles. When an intelligent, educated young woman spends the majority of her time doing cleaning, cooking, laundering, and child-tending, subtle changes occur over the years. By 45 she may have lost much of her alertness, and should she decide to return to the working world, she may find herself in the position of a parolee from an isolated institution, trying to adapt to a strange, frightening, new set of demands. Continuing education programs for older women are developing partly to meet the needs of women who find they need help and moral support in the basics of re-entry.

The myth of normal feminine masochism, or unselfish devotion to others, has encouraged the feeling in many women that child care is a full-time task and that only the mother can accomplish this task without psychological injury to the child. Our laws on child custody bear out this thinking when the natural mother is assumed the better parent until proven otherwise. The task force on Family Law and Policy, however, cites evidence that the average full-time homemaker spends less than two hours per day in direct interaction with her children, including the time spent in conjunction with other

99

duties. For large portions of the day, most children are with age peers, at school, in the neighborhood, and by themselves.

Our stereotype of women's natural role as homemaker has not proved to be to her advantage in terms of mental health. Gurin, Veroff, and Feld (1960) found that single men are less happy, less active, and have lower self-esteem than single women; but married women are unhappier, have more problems, feel less adequate as parents, have a more negative and passive outlook on life, and show lower self-esteem than married men. Also, and perhaps most revealing, married women showed lower self-esteem the longer they were married, while married men did not differ in this respect over time. As long as we have values about how people should run their lives, we will have theories to perpetuate the status quo. As long as we qualify the nature of the relationships between the sexes, then we will find ourselves trying to mold people to fit the theories and priding ourselves on how well we help them to adjust. Under the guise of identifying maturity and mature love relationships, we dictate what love should be. Consider, for example, the choices clinical psychologists have traditionally provided women to meet the requirements of mature behavior. Broverman and others (1970) studied clinicians' ratings of traits of mature men, women, and adults in general. Mature men and mature adults are described by psychologists almost synonymously: independent, objective, active, competitive, logical, and worldly. Mature women are described otherwise: tactful, gentle, tender, religious, neat and quiet. We clinicians seem to have nicely arranged things so that women can never become mature healthy adults in our society without giving up their femininity. The labeling for femininity and masculinity is fraught with prescriptions for approval by men. Being unmasculine is probably an even worse label than being unlovable, although being unfeminine no longer scares women. In fact, being just like a man is often considered a sincere compliment. Sherman (1971), in a review of the concept of femininity, notes that "exaggerated aspects of feminine character development, especially the extremes of dependence and passivity, are associated with incompetence and poor performance as wives and mothers." As early as 1942, Maslow refuted the myth of sexual adequacy associated with extreme femininity when he found that the passive, submissive woman was prone to be less orgastically potent than the assertive, self-assured, more dominant woman.

What does all this mean? Our expectations for adult women have not been very realistic in terms of their capacities, their desires, and their well-being. Psychology has been incredibly slow to integrate the data that has been known about the irrationality of the still existing stereotypes concerning male-female relationships. Fortunately, the role patterns are changing in spite of clinical admonitions not to do so. Judd Marmor (1968) reports that girls today play more vigorously, have greater muscle strength, increased freedom socially and sexually, and are considerably more assertive. Wives and mothers are more dominant in the home, make more decisions, are accepting the role of disciplining children, and are increasingly found in the labor force.

Among the present young generation, there is a new breed that is not afraid of us psychologists. They are not afraid to be labeled pathological, immature, pregenital, or narcissistic. The new wives do not have to nag their husbands to do something; they can do it themselves. The college girl does not have to quit school to put hubby through. She can finish first herself. Babies are being brought to classes and offices by their mothers and also fathers when the sitter does not show up, because adequate inexpensive day care is not a reality yet. These new women and men are not waiting for the institutions to catch up. They are finding their own solutions, experimenting with their own new patterns of relationships, and finding mates eager and willing to help them. Traditional marriage counseling is not relevant to this group. If we are going to develop a theory and therapy to help them in their emotional struggles, we are going to have to first admit that their problems do not fit our conventional values. Our present concepts of love and mental health are going to have to adapt to the new life styles that are already taking form. The new definitions of love will have to make room for a companionship which leaves individual freedom intact and allows for a sharing of experiences and mutual needs rather than a division of needs assigned by sex. Until there is more positive evidence that the present psychological sex roles have a biological base, there

102

is no need to cling to them as inevitable, healthy ideals. Society's need for romantic love leading to conventional nuclear family structures is greatly diminished today, particularly considering the lessened desirability for couples to produce offspring and the increasing length of the life span, with child-bearing and child-rearing years occupying a significantly shorter period of the individual's time. Until we can adequately justify otherwise, the sole reason for intimate relationships should be the desire for mutual satisfactions of whatever characteristics and patterns the couple chooses, and this includes homosexual love. No fixed formula for treating a spouse or lover need apply if alternate choices are to be made available for suiting individual needs.

Dealing with this kind of freedom of choice is another matter. We need to build up confidence in the patients we see by encouraging new relationships in spite of prevailing attitudes, rather than encouraging submission in the name of adjustment. An individual should not be ashamed to seek a freer life, to take the options opening up every day without fear of retaliation and censure. We need to encourage women in particular to refuse to adjust to group pressure, whether from family, roommates, encounter groups, peers, or any others who want to prescribe the way women ought to feel about their lives and their lovers. As Edith DeRham (1965) has said, "Let a woman put her family aside for an instant and the clamor of the righteous can be heard through the land."

We cannot continue to promote the cliches about love's selflessness, the intrinsic satisfactions of caring for another, and the notion of love associated with bowing to another's will. As therapists, one way we can deal with the cultural uncertainties of the nuclear family is by keeping in touch with the current status of the women's rights movement. We can also listen more carefully to what our clients are saying about their relationships and help them prepare for a world with many more options than we and our parents were offered. When Freud (Jones, 1953) admitted that he did not understand what women wanted, he disqualified himself as an authority on the subject. Likewise, any therapist (male or female) who tells a patient "I don't believe in equality for women" or "I don't understand what women want" or "my patients aren't interested in women's rights" should voluntarily disqualify himself from advising women. Love may be here to stay, but it is going to be a different kind of love and we had better keep ourselves tuned in to where it is going. To admit that one is not in love or capable of loving in the traditional sense is admitting a host of demeaning characteristics about one's worth. Love has been equated with maturity, self-actualization, positive reinforcement, and making the world go 'round. Perhaps when our theories can dissociate love from the ultimate of mental health and maturity, individuals can admit temporary or permanent absence of a love relationship without shame or panic, and we will be able to knock love off its virtuous pedestal.

Psychologists have been long using concepts like

love, maturity, femininity, and masculinity in the sense of culturally-approved behaviors. They then decree as pathological any behaviors that deviate from these cultural norms, thereby perpetuating traditional values, often beyond their usefulness. This kind of thinking closes us off from being receptive to differing life styles that violate the current norms, and this rigidity of our theories and therapists is what causes feminists in psychology to protest that "Psychology is part of the problem."

I opened this paper with a quote from *The Prophet* and I would like to close with another:

> "Love one another, but make not a bond of
>   love . . .
> Stand together yet not too near together for the
>   pillars
> of the temple stand apart, and the oak tree and
>   the
> cypress grow not in each other's shadow."

REFERENCES

Broverman, I. K., Broverman, D. M., Clarkson, F., Rosenkrantz, P., & Vogel, S. Sex role stereotypes and clinical judgements of mental health. *Journal of Consulting and Clinical Psychology*, 1970, *34*, 1-7.

De Rham, E. *The love fraud*. New York: Clarkson N. Potter, 1965.

Gibran, K. *The prophet*. New York: Alfred A. Knopf, 1923.

Gurin, G., Veroff, J., & Feld, S. *Americans view their mental health*. New York: Basic books, Monograph Series No. 4, Joint Commission on Mental Illness and Health, 1960.

Jones, E. *The life and work of Sigmund Freud*. Vol. II. New York: Basic Books, 1953.

Marmor, J. Changing patterns of femininity: Psychoanalytic implications. In Rosenbaum, S. and Alga, I. (Eds.) *The marriage relationship-psychoanalytic perspectives*. New York: Basic Books, Inc., 1968.

Maslow, A. Self esteem and sexuality in women. *Journal of Social Psychology*, 1942, *16*, 259-294.

Report of the Task Force on Family Law and Policy, Citizens' Advisory Council on the Status of Women, April 1968.

Sherman, J. *On the psychology of women: A survey of empirical studies*. Springfield, Illinois: Charles Thomas, 1971.

6

Alternatives to Romantic Love

Margaret Horton

> So take away chivalry
> Abolish the family
> But don't, please don't,
> Don't fuck around with love.[1]

ONE OF THE primary obstacles to a sophisticated understanding of love has been semantic problems. The same word, which is ill-defined in the first place, is used to characterize a number of qualitatively different interpersonal relationships. If that were not enough, this same word is made to cover concepts like patriotism (love of country), to need or require (plants love sunlight), and sexual intercourse (make love). In all, the Random House Dictionary (1967) lists twenty-four definitions for "love," as opposed to five for "hate" and four for "indifference."

To confine ourselves to the interpersonal aspects, however, the definition I find most useful is "Love is that condition in which the happiness of another person is essential to your own" (Heinlein, 1961). This seems to capture the essence of the emotion without being overly restrictive.

Given that definition, then, let us take a look at the functions that erotic adult love serves. First there is the social aspect. It is well known that in our society love is a highly positively sanctioned activity. "All the world loves a lover," and people "in" love are readily forgiven for violations of social norms that would otherwise be punished, such as ignoring all that is going on around them. Part of this indulgence is undoubtedly due to the fond memories lovers elicit from the individuals around them. Nevertheless, it remains that love is an activity that is sanctioned by society as such.

Love and marriage are intimately linked in our society, though this was not always true, nor is it true today in other cultures. This link between love and marriage is a key factor in its social significance. Any society, to remain stable, must have a well-regulated and reliable method for bringing up children and thereby assuring a steady flow of new citizens. There are many ways of accomplishing this goal, such as the extended family or community child-care resources, but in the United States, with its cult of individualism and resistance to government intervention, the nuclear family has been the most efficient child-rearing unit available. There are reasons other than the ones cited which are too com-

108

plex for the present discussion. There is considerable evidence that this is changing and that social practices will force institutional change (Slater, 1970; Reich, 1971). In the past, the economic interdependency of the marital partners plus the stresses and rewards of large families were significant forces in cementing the marital bond. However, in the last 50 years, the advantages of having fixed roles for husband and wife have declined: women have begun to have economic power in their own right and the positive sanction for having children has been converted to a negative sanction. Love has had to carry most of the burdens for holding marital relationships together.[2] Thus, the emphasis in marriage has shifted to satisfaction with the love relationship, and the divorce rate has risen correspondingly.

A second segment of society that beams approvingly on budding lovers is the manufacturers of consumer goods. The most phenomenal rip-off of all is weddings, but that is only the beginning. One need only listen to a jewler's ad that urges the teen-age listener to "buy her that pre-engagement ring" to realize that the eyes of merchants light up when they see lovers primarily because they hear the music of cash registers in their ears. Each individual family must have its own vacuum cleaner, blender, dishwasher, garbage disposal, and so on ad nauseam. It might conceivably be argued that if nuclear families need all this, then carried to its ultimate end, merchants should emphasize staying single, because then every *person* would need all this. However, single persons usually realize they don't need all that stuff; whereas in marriage each partner buys it because he thinks the other one wants it. However, businessmen succeed in capitalizing off single persons also because they are more vulnerable to the propaganda that states they are neither sexy nor lovable unless they utilize an enormous number of products ranging from deodorants and toothpaste to late-model sports cars.

A third great force in our society that nudges people into falling in love is the fact that people have to work like crazy to earn enough money to buy all the goods that they need to be lovable. Any person with minimal skills can support himself or herself adequately for a couple of thousand dollars a year. Why would anybody work harder if not for the fact that really desirable things like sexual satisfaction and love are linked in our minds with the possession of material goods. Obviously, to keep the machinery of the economy running smoothly, people must be duped into both producing and consuming these goods. Greenfield argues, in a paper in this volume, that "love" is necessary to induce a man to give away his valued money and possessions to a strange woman and her children. I would say, instead, that the reason men work so hard for material possessions is because they think this will buy them the love they desire.

The personal reasons for being in love are more compelling and better documented than the social. As Casler points out in this volume, one gains access to a sexual outlet, has some measure of security, and is allowed to express dependency needs. One also

110

gains approval, nearly undivided attention, someone to whom it is acceptable to give, and someone to share experiences with. More significant than any of these, love brings relief from the overwhelming loneliness that our society fosters.

So far we have been talking about adult erotic love in general; romantic love is a subcategory which is distinguished by loss of conscious control over one's life and destiny. Romantic love "happens"; it is not brought about; one falls in love. The person is obsessed with the loved one and is unable to concentrate on anything else. The person loses all desire to remain independent, and instead desires to merge and subsume himself into the other. Sovereignty over one's thoughts, feelings, behavior, and destiny are all relinquished (the original escape from freedom).

The advantage to romantic love is that it is exciting; the disadvantages are numerous. A commonly cited criticism of romantic love is that it is too demanding on both the lover and the beloved. John Collier's (1954) short story "The Chaser" illustrates this point. A young man comes into a magic shop seeking a love potion which the old man guarantees him is permanent, will substitute devotion for indifference, admiration for scorn. "She'll want nothing but solitude and you," the old man assures him and continues to describe how jealous she will become, how he will be her sole interest in life, how devotedly she will care for him, and how frantically she will worry if he is a minute late. The young man is rapturous. At the same time the old man is selling him this marvelous potion for the sum of one dollar, he is careful to inform him of the existence of another elixir which will remove the effects of the first. The price of that mixture is $5000.

The second major criticism of romantic love is that it is based on illusion. After all, if you fall in love at first sight, then you cannot have a very realistic notion of the other person. The brisk sale of colognes, make-up, padded bras, padded shoulder jackets, girdles, and elevator shoes demonstrates only the physical aspect of the process of deluding others, and perhaps oneself. Germaine Greer (1971) was not the first to point out that men despise women as a class so much that these illusions are necessary for them to love at all. H. L. Mencken's (1967) statement, "Love is the delusion that one woman differs from another," represents this misogynist point of view. People regularly fall in love with idealizations, then their dreams of perfection are eroded as reality asserts itself. The maintenance of the illusion is even more disastrous to the individuals concerned than would be the consequences if their deceit were discovered. To have a lie accepted as oneself and then to have to live that lie may be poetic justice, but it is certainly a harsh punishment.

The third major problem with romantic love is that it is predicated on a power-based relationship. Shulamith Firestone's (1971) definition of romantic love is, "Love which has been corrupted by an unequal balance of power." As previously mentioned, one of the characteristics of romantic love is the desire of the participants to lose their individuality and merge with the other person. Now if both lovers are merged, nobody is left to take care of business. So one or the other must emerge as the dominant one; in our culture it is usually the man. Furthermore, men and women have different conceptions of love, and it has vastly different significance for them. It has been traditionally accepted that women devote their lives to love and the fruits thereof, whereas this forms a relatively minor part of men's existence. Simone de Beauvoir (1961) presented a brilliant analysis of this phenomenon. This generalization is much less true now (in that men are more able to admit their emotional needs) but it is still a significant force in establishing the domination of men over women. The root problem here is not that love is a vehicle for men to subjugate women; the reverse would be just as odious; the point is that romantic love, by definition, requires that one partner hold a position of power over the other.

These criticisms alone are enough to establish the destructive nature of romantic love. Yet conditions in American society today are such that love is being called upon to fulfill tremendous needs. Popular songs suggest that if we only had enough love, everyone would be happy, there would be no more wars, and President Kennedy would not have been assassinated. A look at the phenomenal success of *Love Story*, a naive, sentimental tale, shows what a responsive chord was struck in the hearts of the public. Love cannot solve the world's problems and should not be asked to. What we need is a more realistic conception of love and its capabilities. What are the alternatives to romantic love?

One form of love that is rarely discussed, and I believe much more widely practiced than people would like to admit, is contractual love. In this, the partners have an agreement, usually unspoken, to love each other as long as the loved one continues to behave in certain ways. The "her" side of the agreement might run something like, "As long as you provide for me and don't beat me or insult me in public, I will love you." His might go, "As long as you clean the house, take care of the kids, and are decent to me when I come home, I will love you." Contractual love can be seen in its most cynical and obvious form where one person marries another (and agrees to love) for financial gain. However, at least part of the popularity of couples living together is due to the fact that the bonds are easily dissolved and little commitment was required in the first place. The positive aspect of this model is that unrealistic promises to love one another forever are not made. However, in this particular form, neither are extensive commitments of any kind made to the other person. Granted, all love has conditional elements (or else it would be masochistic), but this form is a little too calculating for me. After all, we do not stop loving our children even if they do things we disapprove of and refuse to tolerate. While I would not deny the authenticity of a love that diminished after the loved one began behaving intolerably, I would like to see a more sophisticated model, one which

114

places more emphasis on character and less on superficial behavior.

A form of love that is attracting more attention than adherents is various attempts at group love. Books like *Stranger in a Strange Land* (Heinlein, 1961) and *The Harrad Experiment* (Rimmer, 1967) have served as models for persons attempting to escape the restrictions of monogamy. The advantage of this arrangement is that one's emotional and sexual satisfaction need not be tied to one object and source. Of course, one must be prepared to give to an equal number of people. My reservations about this approach are more practical than theoretical. Theoretically, it is beautiful, but so is romantic love. Of course it is possible to love more than one person at a time, but to live together creates problems that are almost insurmountable for people raised in our culture. Sexual jealousy is much more easily overcome than, for example, the desire to control events and to relate in hierarchical patterns. Even those problems could be overcome if the people were committed to each other. I have seen several experimental living arrangements fail disastrously because the persons involved were committed to an ideology rather than each other. The only chance I see for such experiments to succeed is if the people involved first discover the nature of their feelings for each other, then extrapolate to the kind of living arrangement that would be appropriate for them. However, even though these attempts frequently fail, the people who are trying deserve congratulations for their bravery. Individuals in our society need to learn how to live and work together instead of retreating to their own cocoons when problems occur.

It seems appropriate at this point to say something about the love that homosexuals feel for one another. Gay liberation has made many people aware for the first time of the fact that homosexuals want, and are entitled to, dignity in their relationships. In order to discuss this conception of love, I find it necessary to make a distinction between old gay and new gay (although this distinction is not necessarily age-related). Old gay relationships are characterized by stereotyped exaggerations of some of the worst features of male-female relations, particularly role-playing and power aspects. Male homosexuals who take the feminine role appear ridiculous to us partly because we see the behavior as being inappropriate for a male, partly because it is an exaggeration, and partly because the feminine behaviors they imitate are often ridiculous in the first place. Female homosexuals who adopt the masculine role are often characterized by extreme machismo (behavior reflecting patriarchal attitudes) and a "tough guy" image. In the old gay world, relationships were based on the romantic love model and were often so game-riddled that it is doubtful if any true intimacy occurred.

The new gays are a completely different breed. Perhaps because the deficiencies of the romantic model were so blatant in their world they were better able to confront issues, and they have now emerged

116

with a model for love that everyone could learn from. Its basic tenet is the right to love one another with freedom and dignity, a right that heterosexuals seldom have to fight for. One major premise is that role-playing is a game that is inappropriate in a love relationship. Each person should be free to do the things he or she does best without the constraints of stereotypes. The other major point is that love should not involve power plays. Neither partner should be dominant. In actual practice, as usual, the real and the ideal are separated by a considerable gap.

It has seemed to me that female homosexuals have been somewhat better able to realize this ideal then males. I attribute this phenomenon to the extra support available to females from the women's movement, though that may or may not be accurate.

Finally, I would like to discuss the model for love that I like. The word "epigenetic" seems most descriptive of the kind of love I am talking about. (Thanks to Gloria Gordon for this suggestion.) In biology, epigenetic refers to the phenomenon of modifications in an embryo due to environmental influences. Thus, epigenetic love is love that continually changes and grows with time and experience. It combines the best facets of the forms of love previously discussed.

The basic principle is that epigenetic love is founded on a realistic appraisal and acceptance of the other as that person *is*, not as that person *should* be according to someone else's ideals. Rather than falling in love, people grow into it. They gradually come to know one another and learn to love the whole person, not a public image.

A second feature is that unrealistic promises are avoided. Like contractual love, no promises to love forever are made, although other kinds of commitments are. Because epigenetic love is based on enduring aspects of the other, this love has a better chance to survive than a love based on illusion. But people change, and so do their values and goals. What is right for one time may not be right for another.

Third, epigenetic love is not possessive. It is recognized that involvement with others enriches the core relationship. This is not to say that sexual promiscuity or being in love with others is necessarily tolerated. Nor is it to say that jealousy does not exist. But jealousy occurs only when the primary relationship is seen as being threatened. The difference between romantic and epigenetic love is in the degree of involvement with others that is seen as threatening.

The fourth point is that maintaining a relationship takes work. In the past, love stories tended to end at the point where people realized they were in love and they got married; it was assumed that they lived happily ever after. But in real life, this assumption is no longer made. Thus, people now ignore these stories and instead spend hours talking together about their feelings and ironing out difficulties.

Out of the same background as the new gay model, epigenetic thinking arrived at the same conclusion: that role playing is detrimental to the person and to the relationship. Each person should be free

118

to do what they do best and want to do. The maintenance work that no one wants to do is divided functionally, not on the basis of sex. Thus there are husbands caring for the children and wives working on the car. There are also many whose behavior conforms to role expectations, but the decision to behave that way was made after consideration of other alternatives; it was not automatically assumed.

Finally, epigenetic love is dedicated to the proposition that men and women are created equal and that neither should be dominant in the love relationship. This proposition has dual drawbacks in that it is difficult to live up to and that decision-making takes work. But these disadvantages are more than outweighed by the positive results. Every interaction that entails oppressed and oppressor results in feelings that are antithetical to intimacy. The oppressor becomes insensitive and indifferent. The oppressed one uses guilt and dependency to maintain his position. By contrast, with epigenetic love, all this is rejected in favor of true give-and-take and mutual support.

Although there have always been isolated examples of couples who have practiced these principles, the incidence is increasing hearteningly. Furthermore, they are increasingly articulate and vocal about their beliefs. John Dryden (1942) once said, "Love either finds equality, or makes it." That is an alternative to romantic love I would like to believe.

FOOTNOTES

1. Copyright New Haven Women's Liberation Rock Band.

2. Coppinger and Rosenblatt (1968), in a cross-cultural study, found that love was less necessary as a marital bond in societies where spouses depended upon each other for subsistence. Interestingly, Rosenblatt (1967), in another cross-cultural study of 75 societies, found romantic love to be surprisingly predominant in other societies and that "it no longer seems reasonable to state that romantic love is rare across all cultures and occurs in our own culture because of some grotesque cultural pathology (p. 479)."

REFERENCES

Collier, J. The chaser. *In fancies and goodnights*. New York: Bantam, 1954, p. 415.

Coppinger, R., and Rosenblatt, P. Romantic love and subsistence dependence between spouses. *Southwestern J. Anthropology*, 1968, *24*, 310-319.

de Beauvoir, S. *The second sex*. New York: Bantam, 1961, p. 603ff.

Dryden, J. In Mencken, H. L. (Ed.), *A new dictionary of quotations on historical principles from ancient and modern sources*. New York: Alfred Knopf, 1942, p. 1715.

Firestone, S. *The dialectic of sex*. New York: Bantam, 1971, p. 130.

Greer, G. *The female eunuch*. New York: McGraw-Hill, 1971, p. 245ff.

Heinlein, R. *Stranger in a strange land*. New York: Putnam & Sons, 1961, p. 345.

Mencken, H. L. In Woods, R. L. (Ed.), *Modern handbook of humor*. New York: McGraw-Hill, 1967, p. 2077.

Reich, C. *The greening of America*. New York: Random House, 1971.

Rimmer, R. *The Harrad experiment*. New York: Bantam, 1967.

Rosenblatt, P. Marital residence and the functions of romantic love. *Ethnology*, 1967, 6(4), 471-480.

Slater, P. *The pursuit of loneliness*. Boston: Beacon, 1970.

Stein, J. (Ed.). *Random House dictionary of the English Language* (Unabridged). New York: Random House, 1967, p. 849.

7

Homosexuality and
Homosexual Love

James K. Cole

LOVE, IN OUR culture, has a variety of meanings.
Patriotism, parental affection, and a variety of interpersonal and group affiliations have been described
as forms of love. To avoid confusion and in order
to deal with a number of issues which seem to be
relevant to homosexuality, this paper will attempt to
focus on a somewhat arbitrary but relevant definiton
of the concept. Harlow (1971) has identified various
types of love: maternal, infant, peer or age mate,
paternal, child, preadolescent, adolescent, and
heterosexual love. He is classifying love in terms of
affectionate feelings for others and thus distinguishing love from other cultural usage and self-love.
Although Harlow deals primarily with heterosexual
love and its antecedent stages, love, as I am considering it, refers to a similar state—namely, a type of
affectionate feeling or bond between two people at

123

the adult level. Love, as I am using the term, refers to a selective and sustained encounter between two people characterized by mutual erotic pleasure and affection.

Before examining this relationship and relating it to homosexual relationships, I will deal briefly with the selection of this definition within the context of the paper. For many discussions of love, the concept as defined here may not be at all appropriate. For example, many relationships that provide mutual pleasure to the individuals involved may contain little, if any, erotic manifestations, but still could be correctly labeled as love. On the other hand, the term is not restricted to sexual potentialities. Homosexual behavior as a manifestation of erotic arousal is a fact. Judgments and opinions about homosexuality vary considerably among cultures and historically through cultural changes. Love, as conceptualized in this paper, involves components of an affectionate relationship in addition to sexual arousal. The components of love, as defined, include a sustained relationship, selectivity in relationships, and mutual affection. These components are chosen for two reasons. First, these characteristics are frequently ascribed to love relationships in our society. Second, homosexuality has often been characterized as a pathological condition that mitigates against the possibility of these components occurring between homosexual pairs.

A sustained relationship is in contrast to promiscuous sexuality or one-night stands. It imples that a relationship has some basis which promotes a continuous encounter with another individual. For heterosexuals, sustained relationships are promoted and encouraged particularly through the marriage contract or other enculturations, such as "going steady," "pinnings," or engagements in adolescents and young adults. Selectivity suggests that the other person in a love pair is viewed as a special source of attraction in contrast to other potential partners. One person is important above others. If the two components are combined, the implication is that one person is important above others for a significant period or segment of life. Mutual affection implies that the relationship is a two-way street—that the pleasure and affection involved is derived from the reciprocal satisfactions of both individuals and not simply self-serving for one person in the pair. It is important to note at this point that these components have been chosen as a part of the definition of love not because they are necessary components of various types of love relationships or because they are even desirable in all relationships, but primarily because they seem to be components that are accepted and valued in our society as a part of our romantic lore.

Two questions are relevant to relating love to homosexuality. First, are there characteristics about the homosexual personality that would prevent love? Second, are there characteristics of the social context of homosexual life that tend to produce differences between homosexual and heterosexual pairing?

One of the consequences of contemporary society's open willingness to discuss, expound, and exploit human sexuality has been the release of the subject of homosexuality from the realm of the tabooed and unacknowledged. Anyone who is familiar with the literature on sex is aware that a great deal of "hokum" has been perpetuated under the guise of scientific or professional "expertise." Yet, few contemporary attempts to deal with sexuality have generated the degree of nonsense as the literature on homosexuality. In his description of homosexuality, Socarides (1968) manages to include a comprehensive lexicon of labels which have been used to describe the most perverse and evil aspects of mankind: "Homosexuality is based on the fear of the mother, the aggressive attack against the father, and is filled with aggression, destruction and self-deceit. . . . The unconscious manifestations of hate, destructiveness, incest, and fear are always threatening to break through" (p. 8). The homosexual union is described as including "destruction, mutual defeat, exploitation of the partner and the self, oral-sadistic incorporation, aggressive onslaughts, attempts to alleviate anxiety and a pseudosolution to the aggressive and libidinal urges which dominate and torment the individual" (p. 8). Bergler (1957) is even more colorful with terms like "exquisite injustice collector" and "psychic masochist." Bergler implies that heterosexual and homosexual individuals are distinctly different, and that the homosexual is almost a separate species of humanity. For example, Bergler says: "Every 'bisexual' is a true homosexual, with no strings attached." From Bergler's book, it might be concluded that even the most deformed heterosexual has nothing in common with such perversity. At first glance the reader is surprised to find that both Socarides and Bergler view homosexuality as a curable disease. Yet, when the reader is reminded that both are speaking from the viewpoint of a vested professional orientation, i.e., as psychoanalytic therapists, it is not surprising that psychoanalytic treatment is promoted.

A similar but somewhat more rational position is promoted by another psychoanalytic orientation. Bieber (1962) reports on a study of 106 male psychiatric patients diagnosed as homosexual by 77 members of the Society of Medical Psychoanalysis. In this study the view that homosexuality is psychopathological is unquestioned. However, the unfounded assumptions, poor scientific methodology, and biased sampling of the study are severely criticized in detail by Churchill (1967, chap. 12). It will be noted that Socarides, Bergler, and Bieber all promote a "sickness theory" of homosexuality, and later in this paper I will turn specifically to the issue of homosexuality as a form of mental illness.

Fortunately, hysterical outbursts of unfounded assumptions masked by pseudoscientific jargon and a number of more temperate, but scientifically weak studies are not the only sources for understanding homosexuality. However, most current knowledge about homosexuality is at best tentative. Empirical, methodologically sound studies on homosexuality represent a relatively new field of inquiry. Except for some notable exceptions (e.g., the work of Evelyn

127

Hooker in Los Angeles homosexual communities), knowledge about homosexuality has come from clinical populations and is confounded by pathological conditions.[1] A major research project which is currently being prepared for publication has been conducted by the Kinsey Institute. It is based on a large number of homosexuals primarily in the San Francisco area who do not represent a clinical population.

Despite the tentative nature of our knowledge about homosexuality, evidence is beginning to accumulate which makes it possible to understand homosexuality from an orientation that has a reasonable foundation in data. I prefer to define homosexuality in terms of a predominantly sexual preference or orientation toward members of the same sex. A "safer" definition might emphasize homosexual activity or behavior since most of the data on homosexuality are based on empirical measures of behavior. The weakness of this type of definiton, however, is simply the fact that situations (e.g., prison) may be conducive to homosexual behavior among individuals who, from all other indications, have heterosexual preferences. In addition, some individuals with predominantly homosexual arousal tendencies may, for a variety of social or personal reasons, avoid homosexual behavior. Contrary to Bergler's (1957) contention that homosexuality is distinctly different from heterosexuality, the Kinsey Institute studies (Kinsey, Pomeroy, & Martin, 1948; Kinsey, Pomeroy, Martin, & Gebhard, 1953) have clearly noted that heterosexuals and homosexuals are not two discrete populations. Kinsey *et al.*

128

describe the heterosexual-homosexual continuum. One individual may be predominantly homosexual at one point in his life and at another period predominantly heterosexual. Another individual may have both homosexual and heterosexual inclinations while others experience only heterosexual or homosexual preferences throughout their lifetime.

Clinicians, particularly those who believe that sexual identity is the dominant and preemptive force in personality development, have searched for a "homosexual personality."[2] This search seems to be based on the belief that homosexuals and heterosexuals are two distinct types of people and that the distinction is revealed in a wide variety of personality characteristics. With the revelation of the variability in sexual orientations within individuals and across the individual's lifetime, it is not surprising that this search has been largely fruitless. As Bell (1971) pointed out in a recent presentation to a conference on human sexuality, homosexuals and heterosexuals have more in common with each other than they have differences. Of specific interest is the work of Hooker (1958) who used a psychological instrument to compare a nonclinical population of homosexuals and heterosexuals. Basically, the findings showed that the two groups could not be differentiated on the basis of personality variables tapped by the instrument. Possible exceptions might be "traits due to victimization" (Hooker, 1967) which are the result of a hostile environment rather than a homosexual orientation, traits any victimized minority might have.

The Kinsey *et al*. (1948; 1953) studies indicate that a large proportion of the population have experienced homosexual arousal at some time in their lives. Perhaps as high as 10% of the male population have a predominantly homosexual orientation. Kinsey estimates that about 4% of the male population and 2 to 3% of the female population are exclusively homosexual throughout their lives. The accuracy of these statistics can be questioned, but exact statistics regarding the extent of homosexuality and its variations are not essential; what is significant is the fact that homosexuality is a reality and represents a way of life for a significant number of people in society. For many it remains a way of life that will not substantially change.

Since speculation on the etiology of homosexuality is not central to the concerns of this paper, it will be dealt with only briefly. Besides, little is actually known about the factors which are involved in the development of homosexuality. The lack of a precise dichotomy between heterosexual and homosexual orientations and the wide variety and overlapping personality characteristics of the two orientations suggest that homosexuality may derive from a variety of etiological routes. To date there is no clear-cut evidence that some specific factor—genetic, hormonal, or environmental—is directly related to the homosexual orientation. Most authorities seem to emphasize environmental learning factors in the developmental history of the individual. Money, Hampson, & Hampson (1957) suggest an original ambisexual condition in early childhood, followed by the establishment of gender role in early childhood that is similar to the phenomenon of imprinting. Environmental conditioning, however, does not rule out the possibility that biological factors are related to the probability of homosexual preference. Sexual orientations may depend on a variety of interactional patterns rather than the specific characteristics of any one factor. At any rate, the roles of potential biological and environmental factors remain uncertain.

In relating love to homosexuality, a major issue involved in the "selectivity" and "mutuality" components of love is the issue of the "sickness theory" of homosexuality. If homosexuality is a mental disease[3] that disrupts or prevents the development of normal personal and interpersonal functioning, the possibility of adaptive and satisfying love relationships is reduced.

There is a lack of agreement regarding whether or not homosexuality is a mental disease. Socarides (1970) states that homosexuality is a "form of mental illness," a "dread dysfunction, malignant in character, which has risen to epidemiologic proportions." Although others may avoid a "Red under every bed" scare approach, the view of homosexuality as a disturbance of some sort is a prominent view. The highly respected Wolfenden Report[4] (1957), on the other hand, implies that homosexuality cannot be classified as a mental illness according to current knowledge. The final report of the National Institute of Mental Health Task Force on Homosexuality (1969) states: "Homosexual individuals vary

131

widely in terms of their emotional and social adjust-ments. Some persons who engage in homosexual behavior function well in everyday life; others are severely maladjusted or disturbed in their function-ing. There are those whose total life is dominated by homosexual impulses and those whose sexual behavior is just one component in their total life experience" (p. 2). Jerome D. Frank,[5] Professor of Psychiatry at Johns Hopkins University Hospital, says: "In itself a homophile orientation, except for the fact that it precludes procreation, in no way interferes with the full performance of the person's other pursuits as a good citizen." Thompson, McCandless, & Strickland (1971), in a study compar-ing male and female homosexuals and heterosexu-als, found no important differences in personal adjustment or level of self-evaluation. The National Association for Mental Health, in its statement on homosexuality (1970), points out that there are divergent views toward homosexuality but goes on to say: "There is no evidence either in empirical research or in the experience of other countries that homosexual behavior in itself endangers the health of the individual or of society." Kinsey *et al*. (1948) report: "It is difficult to maintain the view that psychosexual reactions between individuals of the same sex are rare and therefore abnormal or unnatural, or that they constitute within themselves evidence of neuroses or even psychoses" (p. 659).

In my own review of this issue, there seems to be a rough correlation between the degree of empirically-based, scientifically-oriented views about homosexuality and the probability that the sickness theory of homosexuality is rejected. Practitioners with a vested interest in treatment and who view homosexuality almost exclusively from personal experience with disturbed populations are more likely to accept the sickness theory. Some reject outright all evidence except that which comes from patients seen in treatment. Socarides (1970) says: "Only in the consultation room does the homosexual reveal himself and his world. No other data, statistics, or statements can be accepted as setting forth the true nature of homosexuality" (p. 1199). It is true that there are homosexuals who have behavioral or emotional disorders just as there are heterosexuals who have problems in living. It is also apparent that many homosexuals suffer great personal agony because of their position in a hostile society. They suffer feelings of guilt, fear of exposure, fears over potential loss of jobs, fears associated with police reactions, or concern over the reactions of family members, parents, or friends. These individuals may frequently find it difficult to adjust to life, but the question remains as to whether the problem is primarily social or personal, whether modifications in social attitudes are needed or changes in the individual's sexual orientation. An interesting finding in the Thompson *et al.* (1971) study is the fact that despite little difference in personal adjustment or self-evaluation between homosexuals and heterosexuals, a higher percentage of homosexuals (30%) had been in psychotherapy than was true of heterosexuals (10%). Thompson *et al.* conclude that the higher percentage reflects social pressure rather than personal maladjustment. Although it is obvious that considerable knowledge is needed, in the meantime it behooves us to relate to all people first as people and not as peculiar sex objects, to respect individual humanity, and not relate to others as a "species apart" who should be eliminated simply because they differ from the majority. Homosexuals are, first, *people* from a wide variety of walks of life, with differing personal tastes, values, needs, interests, and aspirations.

Homosexuality is a major problem in our society primarily because of the amount of injustice and suffering inflicted upon the homosexual and upon those concerned about him. Fear and ignorance are major causes of the problem. The label of mental illness is primarily a moral judgment reflecting a hostile attitude toward the phenomenon; it is not a label based on medical or psychological fact.

In relating the components of love that have been outlined to homosexuality, it is important to consider the social context of homosexual and heterosexual unions. Society supports and sustains heterosexual unions through its mores and institutions. Marriages and family life are highly valued and although alternative routes for human conduct and child-rearing strategies have been proposed, marriage remains as the primary legal interpersonal union for most heterosexuals. Homosexual marriage is not socially sanctioned nor is it legal. Efforts by homosexuals to change this state of affairs have met with considerable hostility. Our culture has been described as homoerotophobic (Churchill, 1967, pp. 82-83). Erotophobic societies tend to fear and repress erotic behavior. Homoerotophobia refers to the specific fears of society about homosexual behavior, these fears, in turn, generating hostile social attitudes and sanctions. Particularly for males, however, a better term might be one which I call "homophiliaphobia." This term is meant to refer to the fear and hostility in our society generated not only by homoerotic arousal but also by threats to the total masculine identity arising from the myths attributed to homosexuality. It is the *male* image or social identity that is threatened by the belief that homosexual males are effeminate. Pomeroy (1969) points out that male homosexuals who display a feminine affectation, identity, or behavioral style (e.g., the "street queen") represent a clear minority of homosexuals. From his extensive research in England, Schofield (1965) hypothesizes that homosexuality has little effect on the development of the personality. Social casualties among homosexuals result primarily from the consequences of social pressure coming from a hostile social environment. Ford and Beach (1951) have documented many societies where homosexuality is tolerated. They point out that societies dominated by Judaeo-Christian values are relatively extreme regarding hostility toward homosexuality.

What is surprising in a society dominated by homoerotophobia (or homophilaphobia) is the remarkable conformity to social values that exists among many homosexuals. In view of social attitudes and pressures, it would be logical to conclude that homosexuals in our society would develop an antisocial orientation. However, Schofield (1965) found no significant differences between a homosexual and heterosexual sample in terms of religion, church attendance, appearance, or broken homes. Homosexuals actually had a high income, and Schofield points out that the homosexual population, if his data are representative, "must be an important economic asset to the country." Similarly, Simon and Gagnon (1969) report that homosexuals, despite a hostile environment, simply do not have an open conflict with society. According to their data, 80% of homosexuals had no trouble with the police and only one-fifth of those who had been in the military had trouble with their military experience.

When the component of a sustained relationship as a part of the homosexual union is considered, it is obvious from the beginning that society does not provide a mechanism (e.g., marriage) that would encourage continuity in a relationship for homosexuals. The fact that homosexuals appear to be more promiscuous than heterosexuals should not be unexpected. Schofield (1965) indicates that homosexual relationships, even in private, are hazardous and subject to consequences such as arrest or blackmail. For many, one-night stands may be safer. Hooker (1969) points out that the urban gay bar world also operates against permanent relationships. In addition to social pressures and subcultural characteristics, homosexual promiscuity may not have the same personal consequences as heterosexual promiscuity. Schofield suggests that homosexual promiscuity produces no illegitimate children and fewer broken marriages. Yet, despite the wide variety of factors which differentiate the probability of sustained unions among homosexuals from sustained unions among heterosexuals, Pomeroy (1969) reports that some homosexuals "develop long-standing emotional relationships" and "live monogamously" for as long as a lifetime, although this is more common in later years. However, in our culture it is questionable whether an index or criterion for homosexual love should be similar to that for heterosexual love. The bad heterosexual marriages that have continued "for the sake of the children" or despite mutually destructive living patterns suggest that a sustained relationship over an adult lifetime is not necessarily a good measure of love for either heterosexual or homosexual unions.

To summarize, when comparing homosexual and heterosexual love, there appear to be some differences, particularly in terms of the likelihood of maintaining a sustained relationship. These differences are primarily the result of social attitudes and social consequences. There do not appear to be personality differences or differences in social values, and there certainly is no evidence that homosexuality in itself involves mental illness which would mitigate against the possibility of mutual affection and selectivity in homosexual relationships. Although the data on the nature of homosexuality do not relate directly to the quality of love relationships between homosexuals, when we ask the question "Can homosexuals love?" we have to conclude:

Why not? Pomeroy (1969) succinctly illustrates this view: "In my twenty years of research in the field of sex, I have seen many homosexuals who were happy, who were participating and conscientious members of their community, and who were stable, productive, warm, relaxed, and efficient" (p. 13).

FOOTNOTES

1. It should not be surprising to see similarities between speculations about the etiology of neurosis and psychosis (e.g., dominant-mother—weak-father characteristics) and homosexuality since the clinician's observations are based on a patient population.

2. Perhaps even more interesting has been the search for "latent homosexuality." The identification of latent homosexuality in patients represents one of the worst examples of professional obfuscation in clinical practice. The base rate expectation from the over-all male population suggests that the probability of finding some type of homosexual residual or inclination may be very high. According to the Kinsey data, half of the male population has had at least one physical experience or arousal that could be classified as homoerotic at some time during his lifetime. Many exclusively heterosexual adult males have had such experiences during adolescence.

3. There is a tendency today to attach the label "mental disease" to many different forms of human and social variability. Alcoholism, crime, radical

political beliefs, group values, religious ecstasy, educational deficiencies, prejudice, poverty, marital problems, etc., have all been labeled as symptoms of "mental illness." One implication is that only the medical field has the right or authority to understand and solve human and social problems, rather than the view that there may be many disciplines or human resources available to understand and solve problems, if indeed there is a problem. If some facet of humanity is a disease, then it follows that it should be eradicated under the auspicies of medical technology. It is interesting that gay liberation is rejecting authoritative dictum. Many homosexuals are proclaiming their right to the dignity of humanity and their right to choose their own life-styles.

4. The "Wolfenden Report" was published in 1957 and represents a comprehensive review of homosexual offenses and prostitution in England. The report was the basis for English law reform in the area of sexual offenses.

5. Personal correspondence, February 25, 1970.

REFERENCES

Bell, A. Paper presented to the Conference on Human Sexuality, University of Nebraska-Lincoln, Fall, 1971.

Bergler, E. *Homosexuality: Disease or way of life?* New York: Hill & Wang, Inc., 1957.

Bieber, I. (Ed.). *Homosexuality: A psychoanalytic study.* New York: Basic Books, 1962.

Churchill, W. *Homosexual behavior among males*. New York: Hawthorn Books, Inc., 1967, pp. 260-291.

Final Report of the Task Force on Homosexuality (E. Hooker, chairman). National Institute of Mental Health, Washington, D.C., October 10, 1969.

Ford, C. S., & Beach, F. A. *Patterns of sexual behavior*. New York: Harper & Bros., 1951.

Harlow, H. F. *Learning to love*. San Francisco: Albion Publishing Co., 1971.

Hooker, E. Male homosexuality in the Rorschach. *Journal of Projective Techniques*, 1958, *22*, 33-54.

Hooker, E. Male homosexuals and their "worlds." Chap. 5 in *Sexual inversion*. Edited by J. Marmor. New York: Basic Books, 1967.

Hooker, E. The homosexual community. Chap. 3 in *The same sex*. Edited by R.W. Weltge. Philadelphia: Pilgrim Press, 1969.

Kinsey, A. C., Pomeroy, W. B., & Martin, C. E. *Sexual behavior in the human male*. Philadelphia: W. B. Saunders Co., 1948.

Kinsey, A. C., Pomeroy, W. B., Martin, C. E., & Gebhard, P.H. *Sexual behavior in the human female*. Philadelphia: W. B. Saunders Co., 1953.

Marmor, J. (Ed.). *Sexual inversion*. New York: Basic Books, 1965.

Money, J., Hampson, J. G., & Hampson, J. L. Imprinting and the establishment of gender role. *AMA Archives of Neurological Psychiatry*, 1957, *77*, 333-336.

Pomeroy, W. B. Homosexuality. Chap. 1 in *The same sex*. Edited by R. W. Weltge. Philadelphia: Pilgrim Press, 1969.

Report of the Committee on Homosexual Offenses and Prostitution (The Wolfenden Report). London: Her Majesty's Stationery Office, 1957.

Schofield, M. *Sociological aspects of homosexuality*. London: Longmars, Green & Co., Ltd., 1965.

Simon, W. and Gagnon, J. H. Homosexuality: The formulation of a sociological perspective. Chap. 2 in *The same sex*. Edited by R. W. Weltge. Philadelphia: Pilgrim Press, 1969.

Socarides, C. W. *The overt homosexual*. New York: Grune & Stratton, 1968.

Socarides, C. W. Homosexuality and medicine. *Journal of the American Medical Association*, 1970, *212*, 1199-1202.

Statement on Homosexuality by the National Association for Mental Health, November 20, 1970.

Thompson, N. L., McCandless, B. R., & Strickland, B. R. Personal adjustment of male and female homosexuals and heterosexuals. *Journal of Abnormal Psychology*, 1971, *78*, 237-240.

Weltge, R. W. (Ed.). *The same sex*. Philadelphia: Pilgrim Press, 1969.

8

Sexual Contact between Patient and Therapist

Charles Clay Dahlberg

My INTEREST IN this subject arose when I heard from a small number of women—not all patients of mine—that they had had sexual relations with their psychotherapists. I noted down some facts about the cases and, over a period of time, quite by accident acquired more cases; a total of nine in about twenty years of practice. I have not included in this list the gossip about the therapist whom "everybody knows sleeps with his patients," but have confined myself to cases based on first-hand information from one of the parties involved.

The topic is such an obvious source of gossip, cartoons, and jokes that it is surprising that more has not been written about it. The object of this paper. is to provoke discussion and clarification of the issues involved in a matter that has too long been kept out of the literature.

143

The rationalizations that therapists offer for sleeping with patients tend to be along the line of it being in the best interests of the patient. Since therapists are human, however, there is little need to speak about the ubiquitousness of temptation nor the remarkable capacity of the human animal to make the unlikely seem plausible.

When I first wrote this paper I stated, "There is no theory of psychotherapy which encompasses sexual intercourse as a psychotherapeutic modality." Since then a paper, "Overt Transference" by James L. McCartney (1966) has been brought to my attention. He defines overt transference as "a visible, audible or tangible muscular or glandular reaction to an inner feeling." Which is to say that some patients (10 to 30%, he estimates) need to do more than just talk about their feelings toward their therapist. They need to caress, fondle, observe, and examine the body of the therapist and have all or some of these activities reciprocated and, in some instances, have sexual intercourse with him. McCartney is quite explicit about this and states that, in some cases in which the patient cannot find an appropriate person outside of the analytic situation to be a surrogate in acting out, an analyst of the opposite sex "may have to remain objective and yet react [sexually] appropriately in order to lead the immature person into full maturity."

At the beginning of the analysis, McCartney explains his method to the patient and appropriate family members. He says the patient may not only

144

say but do anything she wants and he will react appropriately, and that each overt reaction will be fully analyzed and explained. The end result is said to be mature acceptance of heterosexual feelings and actions without reserve or guilt. He seems to be referring only to "positive" transference reactions, since at no place does he mention encouraging such things as violence against the analyst.

It is conceivable that McCartney's method and theory are valid. He reports good results and no complaints. His emphasis on complete objectivity, however, raises some doubts which are dealt with by Fromm-Reichmann (below).

The cases I shall report are not of the McCartney variety; rather, they are cases of neurotic acting out by depressed or sociopathic and frequently grandiose therapists who have lost control of their actions. These therapists come from a variety of backgrounds. Some are very well trained, some less so. Some are analysts, some are not. Some have a medical background and some not. There is no pattern here but, as will be seen later, these people do have some things in common.

I will briefly review some of the literature and then cite cases, each of which deals with different aspects of the problem. The amount of information in each case varies greatly, and some of the case histories must be quite sketchy because of the delicacy of the material. Finally I shall try to make some generalizations.

There has been very little written on the subject.

Freud's attitude on this matter was abundantly clear. It can be summed up adequately from his 1915 paper (1949) on transference love. First Freud commented on "conventional morality and professional dignity" and then he noted "that the patient's falling in love is induced by the analytic situation." He cautioned for control and keeping the countertransference in check because, as he said, "One cannot keep such complete control of oneself as not one day suddenly to go further than was intended."

He noted that, if advances are returned, "it would be a great triumph for the patient but a complete overthrow for the cure" and that "the love relationship actually destroys the influence of the analytic treatment." In his most trenchant statement on the subject he said, "[the analyst] is not to derive any personal advantage. . . . The patient's willingness makes no difference whatever; it merely throws the whole responsibility on [the analyst]." Toward the end of this paper, he expressed concern about the effect of this sexual acting out on the good name of psychoanalysis among the lay public.

Fromm-Reichmann (1950) approached the subject somewhat differently, dealing with it from a practical psychotherapeutic point of view. Although she spelled it out in greater detail, she summed up her attitude when she stated,

> "Therapists have to safeguard strictly against using the patient, actually or in fantasy, for the pursuit of lust so that sexual fantasies . . . do not interfere with the

psychiatrist's *ability to listen"* [emphasis mine].

Fromm-Reichmann put great emphasis on the ability to listen and pointed out that listening was foreclosed if the therapist was not successful in "securing the personal fulfillments in life which he wanted and needed." She carefully noted that "professional relationships between psychiatrists and patients preclude any sort of nonprofessional mutual intimacy." Here she was referring to fantasy. Later statements indicate that she was not so naive as to think that it was all fantasy and that sexual acting out could not occur. In commenting on Ferenczi's experiments on reenactment, she objected to the loss by the therapist of his role as participant-observer "by becoming a gratified participant coactor in relation to the patient's infantile needs."

Two more quotations from Fromm-Reichmann are appropriate here.

> "Most assuredly, the patient should *not* be put into the position of having to reassure the doctor. Fortunately there are patients who are able to see and verbalize this danger. The psychiatrist who is not preoccupied in his quest for gaining security at the expense of his patients may be able to hear their warning."

I am reminded at this point of a very seductive patient of my own who was in the process of changing her attitudes about sexuality. She said, "I'd like to feel that I might be able to make you if it were appropriate, but not while I'm paying you to do something else."

To return to Fromm-Reichmann. She finally summed up her views by stating,

> "There are two potent reasons of a very simple human nature which make love-making and psychotherapy incompatible. The psychiatrist is not a statue, but a creature of flesh and blood. Therefore, he may wish to make love for therapeutic reasons only, but he may respond to the physical aspects of love-making, in spite of himself, as a person and not as a doctor. Should he, on the other hand, invite or not refuse love-making on the part of the patient without evidencing the physical reactions of a human partner with glandular equipment, he may harm his patient even more because this will be a demonstration of the patient's impotence in arousing him, i.e., of inferiority as a sex partner."

That is undoubtedly the nub of the matter.

You may have noted that, in all of the statements quoted in which Fromm-Reichmann spoke in the third person singular, she used the pronoun "he." This may have been accidental but, in my case reports, "he" is invariable.

Ruth Cohn (1966) commented on the therapist

feeling "tested" if the sexual fantasies were actually acted out. Van Emde Boas (1966) has written briefly on the subject and noted that in the medical profession, gynecologists, as might be expected, are the most frequent "targets" for their patients' sexual desires. Closely following are dentists and family doctors. Psychotherapists are lower on the list, but not much lower. In his experience, these people did not fare well as lovers. Their guilt tended to make them subject to premature ejaculation. My own series of cases neither confirms nor denies this.

I shall report a series of nine case histories, most of them quite brief and all of them fragmentary. They cover a course of action that runs from the relatively harmless to the frankly destructive.

CASE 1

Informant: Therapist.

Age: Therapist, late fifties; Patient, about thirty.

Marital status: Therapist, separated—in process of getting divorce; Patient, single.

After several months of treating this patient, the therapist became enamored of her and in some fashion expressed his feelings. Then, realizing that the situation was out of hand, he transferred the patient to another therapist and sought brief treatment for himself while maintaining a social and sexual relationship with her. The relationship broke up a few months after the transfer to the other therapist was established.

This case illustrates the ideal way such a situation should be handled. I have also heard informally of therapists and patients who, caught up in such a situation, have gone for consultation (separately or together) in an effort to gain some understanding of what had happened so that both could put to constructive use in their lives an understanding of the motivations that had led them into this complicated situation. This is indeed a worthy objective but one with which I have had no personal experience. In none of my cases, except for the one just mentioned, have I gotten any evidence that there was an attempt by one or both participants to gain something in terms of personal growth from the experience.

CASE 2
Informant: Therapist.
Age: Therapist, late fifties; Patient about twenty.
Marital status: Therapist, in the process of separating from his wife; Patient, single.

The patient had been in therapy for an unknown period of time before a liaison with the therapist was established. Plans were made for a future marriage. The therapist transferred the patient and got a divorce from his wife. The patient broke off the relationship with her former therapist. He then had a severe, prolonged, agitated depression which seriously interfered with his functioning. I do not know for sure that coitus ever occurred in this case. The fate of the patient is not known.

I think this case illustrates the danger to the

150

therapist when he does not recognize the source of his trouble and attempts to treat himself by acting out.

CASE 3
Informant: Patient.
Age: Therapist, about sixty; Patient, about thirty-five.
Marital status: Therapist, unknown; Patient, single.

In the course of long-term therapy, the patient frequently spoke of being sexually attracted to the therapist who, as the case was drawing to a close, said that no sexual contact could occur during the course of treatment, implying that it might afterwards. When treatment did conclude, patient and therapist went off to a resort for a weekend of cohabitation. The patient considered this a triumph and spoke freely about it. She also reported that the same course of events had occurred with other patients of the same therapist.

I am unable to comment upon the usefulness of the patient's therapy as I did not observe her prior to treatment. Following treatment, however, she was a hard, cynical, and exceptionally materialistic woman. She spoke of her therapist contemptuously. It is hard to see that the sexual experience was useful for her and, since the planned weekend seems to have been covertly in the therapist's mind for some time during treatment, it must have affected his judgment during at least part of the therapy.

151

CASE 4

Informant: Patient and husband.

Age: Therapist, about fifty-five; Patient, early thirties.

Marital status: Therapist, married; Patient, married.

The patient was in therapy for problems related to depression and frigidity. The therapist treated her husband briefly. The patient, a dependent, helpless, seductive woman, induced the therapist to offer evidences of fatherly affection such as parting kisses after the therapeutic hours. These soon turned into more passionate expressions, including fondling, which she accepted ostensibly as evidence of interest and attempts to reassure. The therapist offered to cure the patient's frigidity on a two-week summer vacation with her. The patient panicked at this offer, although she said she was willing to have sexual relations with him in the office.

In her panic, the patient told her husband of the abovementioned events, and the two of them sought legal advice in an effort to bring suit against the therapist. Legal action was never pursued because of the patient's paranoid tendencies, which led the lawyer to think that the case could not be won.

The patient's panic following the offer of a vacation affair quieted under the influence of sedation, and with an enemy (the therapist) against whom she could organize her paranoid system. She did not again seek psychotherapy but was hospitalized a year later following a psychotic break.

This case illustrates a series of therapeutic errors.

It is clear that the therapist did not have any appreciation of the patient's paranoia or of the fragility of her defenses. He was a highly experienced man of good reputation and it must be assumed that this lack of judgment attests to some serious personal problems beyond the grandiosity involved in his alleged offer to cure her frigidity by two weeks in bed. The post-therapeutic organization of her paranoid system and the subsequent course can only allow this case to be considered a therapeutic catastrophe.

CASE 5
Informant: Patient.
Age: Therapist, about forty-five; Patient, late twenties.
Marital status: Therapist, married; Patient, single.

The patient had about a year of hypnotherapy in which she could, however, not be hypnotized and, at the time of her breaking up an intense sadomasochistic sexual relationship, the therapist suggested that sexual contact might increase the transferential involvement with him. The patient readily accepted the suggestion, seeing him regularly for sessions in which she talked about her problems and had sexual intercourse.

She spoke to friends about her unusual therapy. They told her that they thought she was being exploited inasmuch as she was paying for sex; they suggested that this was a reversal of the usual roles.

As there was no alleviation of her personality

problems, the patient sought psychotherapy elsewhere. When she went into treatment with another therapist, the previous one offered to continue to see her for sex; he would not talk about her problems, he said, but he would no longer charge her. The patient continued this arrangement for several months with equanimity. She was mildly concerned by the fact that the former doctor had his office and home in the same apartment, and that she frequently saw his wife and children. She also reported that the therapist spoke about other patients whom he had "treated" in a similar way.

I followed this patient at considerable length. Except for the fact that she did not get any therapy from him, I was never able to see that any great harm had been done. The patient needed warmth, closeness, and relationships with people instead of things. The therapist responded literally with sexual advances—a misguided attempt to deliver what she needed. I assume that sexual feelings are inevitable in intense psychotherapy, but these feelings must be seen as metaphor. Acting literally upon them is at best irrelevant.

The patient said,

> "The fact that I was paying him bothered me a lot, but I couldn't say anything to him about it or make any complaint because I needed him so much and I didn't want him to stop seeing me."

She gradually cut down the frequency with which

she saw him therapeutically and then eased out of the relationship by getting into treatment elsewhere. The sexual relationship lasted for about eighteen months (also gradually diminishing) while she was actively working on her problems and learning to form more meaningful relationships.

CASE 6
Informant: Patient.
Age: Therapist, forty-eight; Patient, thirty-five.
Marital status: Therapist, single; Patient, single.

This male patient had been seeing a therapist twice a week for a period of five years. For the last six months before he came to me for a consultation, he had also been seeing another therapist once a week. The first therapist did not know about the second one. I do not know if the second knew about the first.

The patient considers himself to be an unsuccessful homosexual because he cannot find love. He described his mother as basically hating him, and he felt that he was her rival for the father. His mother was a largely bedridden hypochondriac, and the patient was the housewife for the father—shopping, preparing the meals, and so forth. He has had few intimate experiences in his life. He respects the second therapist much more than the first because he is straightforward and not protective.

The patient says that his first therapist occasionally touches him, placing a hand on the patient's knee or arm. The patient finds this offensive because in general he hates to be touched, but he says that his therapist convinced him that there is a need for it in order to help him overcome his dislike for being touched.

More important is the following: The patient has occasionally gone to "gay" bars where he has run into his first therapist, who has engaged him in conversation and "groped" him. This provoked intense anxiety in the patient. When he brought up the subject during a session, the therapist told him that certainly any sexual contact between patient and therapist during a treatment session was out of the question, but what went on out of the office was an entirely different matter. The patient could neither accept nor reject that statement. He knew, however, that there was something illogical about it.

He first went into treatment because of intense anxiety. This diminished but he then became plagued by feelings of emptiness and depression. He has also been impotent and feels unattractive.

The therapist in this case is obviously confused. The idea that what goes on outside the office does not carry over into the office is the feeblest kind of rationalization. If I understand what the patient is speaking about when he mentions his feelings of emptiness, depression, and impotence, he is saying he has again failed and been failed, and that exploitation is what life is all about. His second therapist, whom he described as straightforward and not protective, may be able to rescue him from that gloomy conviction.

156

CASE 7
Informant: Patient's husband.
Age: Therapist, over forty; Patient, thirty.
Marital status: Therapist, unknown; Patient, married.

The husband of the woman in this case is also a patient. His symptoms are impotence, anxiety, and depression. He is also phobic. He has had over 300 hours of therapy over five or six years. His therapy has helped him get out of the doldrums and function better and, as he says, "got me on my feet."

After three years of treatment, the husband got into what he described as a "sticky" relationship with his therapist. The wife, in an effort to clarify some internal and intramarital problems, went to his therapist for a consultation and the latter then took her on in treatment. After two years of treating the wife while continuing to treat her husband, the therapist had a brief affair with the wife. That ended the therapy for both of them.

The husband went into a depression for several months and eventually came out of it. He felt that he had been seriously betrayed by his therapist but he said, "I don't mind the sex so much since both my wife and I have had affairs since our marriage."

He has had a number of periods of impotence throughout his life. It was again a problem when he consulted me.

For some reason or other, this man was not as bitter as I would have expected him to be, perhaps because he and his wife both had the good sense to

157

get out of therapy as soon as they knew they were being exploited. Actually, the husband's therapy seems to have been fairly successful. It is too bad that the therapist destroyed it. He might even have been able to treat the wife while treating the husband. What happened to his judgment when he thought he could get away with sleeping with her is not known to me.

CASE 8
Informant: Patient.
Age: Therapist, forty-seven; Patient, thirty-seven.
Marital status: Therapist, unknown; Patient, single.

This woman had had treatment over an undetermined period of time and, after it ended, she had a brief affair with her therapist. I do not know why she originally went into therapy, but she became quite anxious after the affair ended and, not long after, she returned to the therapist for a consultation. He took her back into treatment and discouraged her in her desire to transfer to another therapist. She agreed to return but was quite distrustful of him. The second course of treatement went on for two years while she was having a homosexual affair. This in itself indicates that something was wrong in the transference. He finally agreed that she could go to another therapist, but told her she should not reveal her affair with him.

She resented the entire incident and felt that she had been exploited. Going to bed with him was all right, she said, but he should not have taken her back into treatment. She was angry and unable to work out her feelings.

She later learned from a friend of hers that the latter had also been through somewhat the same course of events with the same therapist.

This patient's statement that she was distrustful about analysis was an understatement. The affair with her therapist and his rigid control over her, motivated by his fear of exposure, threw her into a homosexual regression. She came to me because she had heard that I give LSD. At that time, only desperate people came to me for LSD treatment.

CASE 9
Informant: Patient.
Age: Therapist, about forty-five; Patient, about twenty-two.
Marital status: Therapist, separated and getting a divorce; Patient, divorced.

The patient had been in therapy for about a year. She was greatly attracted to her therapist, which she expressed freely. The therapist suggested that they meet for a drink outside of the office. The patient was hesitant but accepted his reassurances. The meeting led to further dates and, eventually, to bed. After a few months, the therapist told the patient she no longer needed therapy; he terminated the treatment while he continued to see her socially. Shortly thereafter they married. When they decided following the marriage that she again needed treatment, he made her promise not to tell her new

TABLE 1
Data on Cases Discussed

Case	Informant	Age		Marital Status	
		Therapist	Patient	Therapist	Patient
1	T	55±	30±	Separated, getting divorce	Single
2	T	55±	20±	Separated, getting divorce	Single
3	Pt	60±	35±	Unknown	Single
4	Pt and husband	55±	32	M	M
5	Pt	45±	28	M	Single
6	Pt	48	35	Single	Single
7	Pt's husband	40±	30	Unknown	M
8	Pt	47	37	Unknown	Single
9	Pt	45	22	Separating, ultimately divorced	Single

therapist how their relationship had begun. A few years later, as the marriage deteriorated, the patient said that she had reason to believe he was dating one or more of his patients.

This case combines all the worst elements of a situation of this sort. The patient went on to years and years of therapy, several marriages, and untold acting out, including an almost successful suicide attempt. It is clear that this therapist was out of control; he allowed his own needs to interfere with his therapeutic judgment, and he was willing to sacrifice a former patient, then his wife, to protect his reputation. It should be mentioned that he sent his wife to his own former analyst, who had not been told about this case even though the therapist was in training analysis at the time he treated her. The reason he sent her to him was that he felt his wife would be afraid to injure his reputation by telling the facts to his former analyst, and also that the training analyst would be deterred from speaking about the situation if he did learn the facts. The therapist was right. The analyst did not learn about these events until several years after the divorce. Obviously, having to keep this secret interfered with her treatment.

Table 1 assembles the salient information about the nine cases discussed above. What seems to me to be informative about the chart is that, where we have the information, the therapist is always over forty, from ten to twenty-five years older than the patient, always a man, and with exception of the homosexual (Case 6), the patient is always a young

female. In three cases where we have enough information, the therapist is also clearly in a somewhat
difficult heterosexual situation. He is either separating from his wife or they were recently divorced. I
suppose that what the latter adds up to is that people
who have some unfulfilled need are more likely to
succumb to temptation. That gets us back to Fromm-
Reichmann.

There is not enough information here to make
any diagnostic or psychodynamic formulations about
either the patients or the therapists, but I would like
to offer some speculations on the matter of age. It
is a common observation (and possibly true) that
men tend to roam as they reach middle age. It is
also true that therapists caught up in their offices
have less opportunity to meet young women (other
than their patients) than do many other men.

And there is something else to consider.
Remember that many of these cases go back quite
a way in time. All of the therapists, with the possible
exception of the one who handled Case 7, made
their career choices before World War II, when
psychotherapy was not a very popular field. I do not
know as much about the men and women going into
the field nowadays, but a composite picture of the
person who chose to practice psychotherapy
between, say, 1930 and 1945 would be of a fairly
unusual person. He would be rather withdrawn and
introspective, studious, passive, shy, intellectual,
perhaps intellectually adventuresome but not physically so. Among other things, this adds up to being
unpopular with the opposite sex. None of this, of

162

course, stops a person from having fantasies of sexual conquests—it may well encourage sexual fantasies.

When my composite psychotherapist got into practice, he found himself in the unusual position of having women attracted to him—and saying so. For the shy young man, this is a common and persistent fantasy. It is well known that when an old and persistent fantasy is finally realized it is an extremely powerful force and can test a person's will.

When we speak of acting out as I have, we must ask, "Acting out what? What is the fantasy that is being acted out?" The fantasy, I suggest, is of being young, attractive, and having beautiful girls throwing themselves at you without having to take the chance of being rejected by being the one who makes the first move.

Perhaps that is why there are no women therapists in my collection. Their patients have oedipal fantasies about them but those tend to be more strictly maternal; they do not want to go to bed with their analysts in reality. Besides, therapists are older people, and men do not seem to want older women to the same degree that women want older men. I am suggesting that at least part of the reason I have no evidence of women therapists sleeping with male patients lies in lack of opportunity. Perhaps this formulation is unfair.

It would be foolhardy to attempt an over-all psychodynamic generalization on such a subject as patient/therapist sexuality. There are undoubtedly many complex factors involved. But the three cases cited of men in the throes of a marriage breakup in middle age or later do lead to some speculations about depression as a factor in sexual acting out. It can be assumed that depression is usual when there is the loss of such an important relationship. Sexual acting out is also common at such a time. Bibring's (1953) hypothesis that depression is essentially a response to deprivation from a loss is pertinent here. Jacobson (1953) describes a specific ego weakness in depression that is manifested by a decreased tolerance to frustration and disappointment.

With the breakup of a marriage, a loss is crystalized. Depression ensues. Frustration tolerance is diminished—in part, at least, because frustration is increased. Acting out of regressive sexual fantasies is thus more common because of the increased need and the increased freedom to do so. If other opportunities are limited, acting out may occur with patients.

It is probable that the best sexuality is always regressive to some degree, in the sense that more vivid and various sensations occur if one can comfortably give oneself up to infantile and childish forms of tactile sexual expression (oral and anal) as part of the sexual act. The sensual is only one part of the mature sexual relationship and is genetically the earlier. The more mature element is emotional. It is hard to see much in the way of mature emotional involvement in the cases I have described or how McCartney's method with its emphasis on objectivity (nonemotionality) could lead to maturity.

Another regressive element is grandiosity. In its

most blatant form, this is exemplified by the therapist who was going to cure his patient's frigidity on a two-week holiday. More important, though, is the unspoken theme that runs through all of these cases—that the therapist's sexual attentions are what the patient really needs.

It may be that these nine therapists really were God's gift to women, but that is doubtful. In my experience in treating the wives and sweethearts of therapists (none of these cases), I have never gotten any information to convince me that people in our profession were remarkably great lovers. It is more likely that these nine were simply ordinary aging men in a depressive period who somehow let themselves be convinced by their patient's fantasies that they might recapture a real or fantasied youth.

The themes that come through from these patients' feelings are of triumph, betrayal, and exploitation. Certainly some of the women are triumphant—it's a conquest and they've done the impossible. They have gotten some power. They have knocked the doctor off his perch. Here again a fantasy is realized.

The first dream one patient reported was of her analyst turning into a huge dog with whom she had intercourse and tamed. Seven years later as the analysis was ending, she dreamed they went to bed together and it was nice. She said it had to happen to "dot the i." She was glad it was only a dream.

Another patient—a psychologist—who used sex to reduce her anxiety with men said, "I know that therapists don't do it, but somebody must have or

165

Fromm-Reichmann and Freud wouldn't have warned against it. I can't stop thinking it might happen."

I think the lesson from these two examples is that, if we encourage our patients to fantasize and report their fantasies, we must make it crystal-clear that their fantasies will be respected and not acted upon.

When patients' fantasies are acted upon by therapists, the patients feel betrayed—the second of the feelings patients most often report. The first was triumph.

They also feel exploited—and they are. It boils down to the question: Who is the therapy for? From his work the therapist may get the ancillary satisfactions of earning a living, doing a good job, helping, and sometimes learning. These must be enough. The patient comes because he needs help—an admission of weakness. He is encouraged at times to be weak. This imples that the therapist is strong enough, at least, not to take advantage of his patient's weakness. Irrationality is encouraged only because the therapist is the temporary repository of rationality. Anything less is exploitation. It really is not fair play.

Winnicott (1965) has not written specifically about sexual relations between patient and analyst, but he alludes indirectly to the subject in some of his articles. He gets to the heart of the problem in an article on countertransference first published in 1960. "Professional work," he says, "is quite different from ordinary life." He goes on to describe the Hippocratic Oath as giving a picture of an idealized man. "Yet

166

that is how we are when professionally engaged." He quotes Freud's recognition that the analyst is *"under certain strain in maintaining a professional attitude"* [Winnicott's italics] and adds, "The psychotherapist must remain vulnerable, and yet retain his professional role in his actual working hours." In other words the therapist must remain human but try to *behave* ideally.

Winnicott states that the patient is not well served by the

> "unreliable men and women we happen to be in private life. . . . The professional attitude is rather like symbolism, in that it assumes a *distance between the analyst and patient*. The symbol is in a gap between the subjective object and the object that is perceived objectively."

Later Winnicott refers to the analyst's "technique, *the work he does with his mind*" as being between the analyst and his patient. And he adds:

> "The important effect of the analyst's own analysis in this connection is that it has strengthened his own ego so that he can remain *professionally involved*, and this without too much strain." [Winnicott's italics]

There is no denying that a patient can arouse the therapist's anxiety, hostility, or sexuality. Indeed, in small amounts, these and other emotions should be aroused. What is at issue is how the therapist should behave verbally and physically when so aroused. The overriding principle must always be that anything that the therapist does should be in the patient's best interests or at least so calculated as not to harm the patient. Sexual acting out with a patient cannot be in the patient's best interests for, as Winnicott would say, the "gap" between patient and therapist is filled.

Before presenting this paper, I sent copies to a number of colleagues, many of whom have been kind enough to offer helpful comments. The most frequent criticism has been that my data on the cases are too sketchy to allow for an adequate understanding of the dynamics and motivations. I agree. I have given what I can without betraying confidences. By and large, I have given all that was available that I considered relevant. In the two cases where the informant was the therapist, it might seem I would have more information; but I do not. In one of these cases, the therapist spoke to me to explain what was a well-known situation. He did not confide in me as a therapist. In the other case where the therapist was the informant, he seemed to be talking because he could not help it, and I was a friend and willing listener. He seemed to be suffering from an agitated depression at the time and for some months thereafter. I hope this presentation will encourage *better* case reporting of these incidents.

The therapist's job is fraught with difficulties. It is the hardest kind of work, and I will not belabor Winnicott's point. He makes it well. Those of us who are willing to practice our profession do so because we find sufficient rewards that offset the difficulties. Raymond Sobel[2] says (and I agree) that the determinants of whether the therapist acts out are his inner states rather than the seductiveness of the patient. The latter is always with us. At least in part, the answer to this problem is in increasing personal awareness through reanalysis and some sort of system of checks on countertransference—he even suggests a routine check somewhat as Freud suggested analysis every five years.

Another correspondent compared the sexual exploitation with that of "stealing" from a patient by keeping him in treatment longer than necessary and using patients to further our research or training ambitions. Here again I cannot but agree, but I also think there is a difference. The sex act in our culture is the prototype of the intimate relationship. Like it or not, the act carries that significance; and for that reason the exploitation involved, while perhaps being ethically similar to the situations this correspondent cited, strikes deeper into the core of the human personality and therefore is potentially more damaging to the persons involved. The therapists in my case reports have not always come off unscathed. This is not a simple matter of one person exploiting another.

It was also said that there are many therapeutic sins—laziness, pride, greed, and anger among them—and that these all have their consequences. I disagree with this criticism. Aside from the difference I have already mentioned between sexual acting out and these other errors, there is the fact that sexual acting out cannot be reversed. Once done, it remains a fact between the participants. Laziness on a particular day like any of the other sins at least contains within it the possibility of being reversed on a subsequent day.

What is most bothersome about these cases, I suppose, is that it is too easy to sleep with a patient. They come for help and must put their faith in us. They have no alternative. If they hold back too much, there will not be any therapeutic alliance and there will not be any therapy. The cards are all in our hands.

Since the cases reported relate in large measure to people who made a complaint, it can be asked: How many are there who do not complain—who do not feel they are hurt or perhaps, as in McCartney's cases, even think they were helped by their therapists' sexual intervention? This is a worthwhile question and could be answered, at least in part.

What I am proposing is a Kinsey-type survey of therapists and patients to probe into the circumstances and results of sexual acting out and near acting out. What was the nature of the interpersonal dynamics when temptation was strong but resisted, strong but not resisted, and what was the outcome? This would be a tough job, but it could be done.

It must be obvious where my feelings lie. Perhaps my comments will be tempered somewhat by the following personal communication from Mary White Hinckley.

"The allergenic quality of the subject is understandable because who hasn't had fantasies or dreams about patients? The lack of acting out by most psychiatrists doesn't protect them from guilt and fear of exposure, since there is so much that is unconscious in each one of us. If only there could be an anonymous survey of 200 psychiatrists, including dreams, fantasies, and acting out; I suspect that the compulsive sexuality is no higher than in middle-life men who sleep with their secretaries. Psychiatrists just don't have secretaries? The need to give and receive tenderness is especially great in the beginning-to-fail middle years. With diminishing self-worth, is it not more possible to want to give tenderness to someone who is sad or needing 'help'? One could predict that some would end in bed, and some even in marriage. Nurses and social workers often can sublimate by being closely helpful—and some become personally involved to the degree of 'marriage,' hetero or homo.

"Anything goes, except between doctor and patient, for the reason that it is often so cruel, as you have demonstrated so very well. Doctors need help when facing basic loneliness and failure, for 'something *can* be done about *that*' (Harry Stack Sullivan)."

AFTERWORD

Since the above was first published I have received numerous communications from colleagues telling of similar cases they knew about. I have also seen two patients who had happened to see the article and wanted help in understanding how they had gotten trapped in such confusing and destructive sexual relationships with their therapists. There may be some wry humor in the fact that one of the patients found the article in her therapist's waiting room.

All the cases are similar to the ones I described and illustrate the antitherapeutic qualities in relationships involving role confusion and distortions of love. One patient was especially enraged at the conspiracy of silence on such matters within the profession. Her affair happened thirty years ago and she was still obsessed with it.

FOOTNOTES

1. With a few changes most of this article was originally printed in *Contemporary Psychoanalysis*, Vol. 6, No. 2, Spring 1970.

2. Personal communication.

REFERENCES

Bibring, E. The mechanism of depression. In P. Greenacre (Ed.), *Affective disorders*. New York: International Universities Press, 1953.

Cohn, R. C. The sexual fantasies of psychotherapists and their use in psychotherapy. *J. Sex Res.*, 2:219, 1966.

Freud, S. Further recommendations in the technique

of psychoanalysis; observations on transference love in *Collected papers, Vol. II*. London: Hogarth Press, 1949.

Fromm-Reichmann, F. *Principles of intensive psychotherapy*. Chicago: University of Chicago Press, 1950.

Jacobson, E. Contributions to the metapsychology of cyclothymic depression. In P. Greenacre (Ed.), *Affective disorders*. New York: International Universities Press, 1953.

McCartney, J. L. Overt transference. *J. Sex Res.*, 2:227, 1966.

Van Emde Boas, C. Some reflections on sexual relations between physicians and patients. *J. Sex Res.*, 2:215, 1966.

Winnicott, D. W. *The maturational processes and the facilitating environment*. New York: International Universities Press, 1965, pp. 158-165.

9

Unhealthy Love: Its Causes and Treatment

Albert Ellis

LET ME START out with a few of my own prejudices. I have been engaged in research on the subject of love—and I mean love, not just sex—since 1938; that is, almost thirty-five years. My first attempt at a Ph.D. thesis was on the love emotions of college girls; and although Columbia University did not let me proceed with this particular topic (*because* it was on love, and hence closely related to sex), I nonetheless completed the study myself and published it in a series of papers in psychological and sociological journals (Ellis, 1949a, 1949b, 1949c, 1950).

Then I became a psychotherapist and a well-known sexologist. In the latter capacity, I dealt partially or obliquely with love and published a good many articles and books on the subject (Ellis, 1954, 1958, 1960, 1963). In the former capacity, I have dealt with problems of love almost every day for well over a quarter of a century. For it is the basic problem of love—how much do I accept and respect myself and how much do you care for me?—which makes the world go round; and even the so-called sex problems (such as those of impotence, frigidity, and sex deviation) are basically problems of human worth and worthlessness (or self-love)—as I have shown in many of my writings on psychotherapy (Ellis, 1957, 1962, 1971, 1972; Ellis and Gullo, 1971; Ellis and Harper, 1961a, 1961b).

There are many healthy or normal aspects of love, as a great many authorities on the subject have pointed out (Finck, 1887; Maslow, 1953; Montagu, 1953; Grant, 1957; Levy and Munroe, 1938; Ortega y Gasset, 1960; Sorokin, 1954; Stendhal, 1947); there are also many unhealthy or abnormal aspects of love (de Rougemont, 1940; Lucka, 1922; Reik, 1945). I, like Casler, shall deliberately focus on some of the unhealthy aspects. For love is a huge subject, and there is never time or space to cover all its ramifications. Kremen and Kremen (1971) have recently discussed romantic love and idealization from a largely psychoanalytic view and Salzman (1971) has discussed infatuation and dependency love but from a somewhat less orthodox frame of reference. To some extent, they repeat the observations of Fromm (1962), who has incisively analyzed some of the self-defeating elements of in-lovedness and loving. Starting from a highly antipsychoanalytic framework, and sticking largely with clinical data, I shall now give my own analysis of unhealthy love, as well as what can be done to help individuals who are afflicted with this problem.

Most human disturbance is a form of *demanding-ness*. The individual who loves "neurotically" or "psychopathologically" (or, at times, "psychotically") does not merely *want* or *prefer* to be involved intimately with another person; he *demands, dictates, insists,* or *commands,* in a highly absolutistic manner, that (1) he find an unusually attractive individual, usually of the opposite sex; that (2) he act exceptionally well and impressively with this person; that (3) this individual love him completely, devotedly, and lastingly; and that (4) he loves this person in an intimate, deep, and abiding fashion. He may, in addition, have various other demands, such as, that this person whom he discovers and whom he (or she) intensely loves be available (that is, not legally tied to someone else), live nearby, have similar values and goals to his own, be a great sexual partner, et cetera.

If the individual's goals, aims, and purposes about loving and being loved were *wishes*, that would be fine and healthy. But if they are, as they ever so often are, absolutistic dire needs or mandates, if they are incorporated in the utter necessity that they *should, ought,* or *must* be achieved, then that is not fine or healthy; *that* is the essence of emotional disturbance. Let me illustrate with the case of a woman I recently saw who, in spite of her unusual comeliness and intelligence, had a long history of failures in love and insisted that she never had had a reasonably good affair for any length of time and was sure

177

that she was incapable of achieving or maintaining one. She was consequently anxious, depressed, and angry.

I was quickly able to demonstrate to her that her emotional problem—that is her anxiety, depression, anger, and inability to maintain the kind of deep emotional involvement that she said she very much wanted to maintain—could probably best be understood within the A-B-C model that is used in rational-emotive psychology. At point A, the Activating Events, she was finding great difficulty in relating intensely and enduringly to a suitable man; and at point C, she felt the emotional Consequence of despair, panic, anger, and hopelessness. As is almost universal, in cases like this, she flatly stated, during our first session, "Because I am having so much trouble in achieving a long-term relationship with someone I really respect and love, and because I am convinced that I probably never will, this has made me very depressed."

"Oh, no," I immediately interrupted as I frequently do in instances of this kind, "that's not true. You have just made a magical jump—from an external situation to an inner feeling. And, since there is, as far as we know scientifically, no magic in the universe, your statement is a non sequitur. It just isn't so."

"What do you mean?" she asked.

"Well, you're saying that an Activating Event, at point A—the fact that you're having trouble achieving a long-term relationship and the possibility that you will never achieve the kind of relating that you

178

want—is causing a feeling in your gut, an emotional Consequence, at point C. But how could this be? How could *any* Activating Event, or noxious stimulus that is happening to you, cause you to feel something inside you—unless, of course, it were a physical force impinging on you? And even then it would only cause, directly, physical pain; and you would still have to *react*, emotionally, to that pain."

"Do you mean, then, that A *can't* cause C, and that *nothing* can upset me emotionally?"

"Yes, that's just what I mean. Only *you* can upset yourself. And you do so by convincing yourself something at B, your Belief system. What is more, when you're intensely upset—feel depressed, for example—you invariably convince yourself of some utter nonsense, some magical Belief, at B."

"And what is that?"

"Oh, I think I know exactly what that is—for I can figure it out, most of the time, on the basis of my therapeutic theory. But first, let's see if you can guess what sane or rational Belief you convinced yourself of, at point B, just before you thought of the insane or irrational Belief."

"Rational Belief?"

"Yes, rational Belief about what was occurring at point A. It's on the order of, 'I am having a great deal of difficulty in achieving and maintaining a long-term involvement with a man I care for, and that is. . . . ' That is . . . what?"

"That is awful!"

"No, that's your irrational Belief! It's interesting how so many people, just as intelligent and educated

179

as you are, tell me their irrational Belief and think that it's rational. But we'll get back to that in a minute. But first, what *rational* Belief, rooted in empirical reality, do you think you told yourself immediately *before* you gave vent to this irrational one?"

"Mmm. I. . . . I really don't know."

"You do know. You're just not thinking about it. You're probably telling yourself, right now, *another* irrational Belief that's blocking your thinking."

"You mean, 'Isn't it awful that I can't think of this rational Belief he wants me to locate!' "

"Exactly! But let's get back to the rational one. What would *anyone* in your position tell herself, if she wanted very much to get in a long-term involvement and she was having great trouble doing so? 'I have great difficulty relating permanently to a man and that is. . . '?"

"Disappointing?"

"Right! That is disappointing; that is unfortunate; that is deplorable; that is disadvantageous; that is too bad! All these kinds of things. And if you stuck, stuck rigorously *only* to that kind of rational Belief, that it is disappointing and unfortunate but not *more* than that to be unable to relate to a man, how would you then feel?"

"I . . . I suppose I'd feel, well, terribly sad."

"Right again. You'd feel quite sad, sorry, regretful, annoyed, or inconvenienced. For it *is*, we could justifiably say, most unfortunate if you don't relate well to a man, and perhaps never will; and you'd better feel appropriately sad and annoyed about that. But,

180

of course, you feel much *more* than that: you feel very depressed. Now what *ir*rational, empirically un-validatable Belief would you have to feel, again at point B, for you to create this inappropriate feeling?"

"Why is it *in*appropriate for me to feel de-pressed?"

"For several reasons. Although sorrow over not relating might prod you to do more to relate, depression normally won't: it will cause you to be inert, to give up, and to feel that you *can't* possibly relate. Hence, it is dysfunctional or self-sabotaging. Moreover, depression almost always includes self-downing or self-pity. Just answer my question about what your irrational Beliefs are, and I think you will see."

"You mean my irrational Belief about not relat-ing?"

"Yes, in addition to your rational Beliefs that it is unfortunate and disappointing not to relate."

"Well, uh, I guess, uh, that I never *will* be able to relate."

"Yes, that's right. That is an irrational Belief, because it's unprovable. You can prove that you haven't ever related well; and that you *may* never be able to do so. But how can you ever prove that you can't *possibly*, under any conditions, *ever* relate?"

"Mmm. I guess I can't."

"But what else are you irrationally Believing? There's something else even more important than 'I never *will* be able to relate.' "

"Let me see. Uh. Oh, yes: and it's *awful* if I never do so!"

"Right! That's the main villain: that *awfulness* that you are creating in your head. Because you could rationally believe that you haven't related and you most probably never will, but not believe that it is awful. When you do believe that anything you do (or don't do) is awful, it's highly irrational. Why?"

"I don't know. It certainly *seems* awful! Especially if I find out that I never do, actually, relate to any man."

"Yes, but just about anything that you *think* is awful will *feel* awful to you. That's the way the human being works: whatever she very strongly thinks or believes she tends to feel. That doesn't prove a damned thing except that she does have a feeling. But why *is* it awful if you never relate to a man?"

"Mmm. I can't really say."

"Nor will you ever! Because this is a completely magical, unprovable hypothesis. For when you say 'It's awful (or horrible or terrible) if I never relate,' you mean (1) 'It's very inconvenient or handicapping,' as we've already stated and (2) 'It's *more than* one hundred percent inconvenient or handicapping!' Now, how is that possible? Could *anything* that happens to you be *more than* one hundred percent unfortunate or inconvenient?"

"No, I guess not."

"And, again, when you call a thing *awful* you mean (1) 'It's very inconvenient,' and (2) 'Because it's very inconvenient, *it shouldn't exist!*' Well, is there anything in the universe that, because it is terribly incon-

182

venient to you, *should* not, *ought* not, *must* not exist?"

"No, not if it *does* exist."

"Exactly! Whatever exists exists. No matter *how* displeasing failure to relate is for you, if that's what always occurs that's what always occurs. It's silly and grandiose, to say that it *shouldn't* occur."

"Are you saying, then, that if I give up all *awfulness* and accept the reality that when obnoxious things exist there's no reason why they *must* not exist, I won't be bothered at all about being rejected by males I like and about failing to relate for a long period of time to any of them?"

"No, I'm not saying you won't be bothered *at all*; I'm saying that under those conditions you won't be bothered *unduly, irrationally, self-defeatingly*. You'll still be extremely sad and sorry about not relating; but you won't depress yourself about it. And you'll work your head off to rid yourself of this annoying condition—*because* you are bothered about it and want to eliminate it—and do your best to relate."

At the same time that I was showing this woman that her lack of relating was not causing her to be severely depressed but that *she*, with her irrational Beliefs *about* this deplorable state of affairs, was depressing herself, I also showed her that her anxiety and anger were similarly self-caused. To make herself anxious, she was rationally, again, saying that it would be most unfortunate if she failed to relate; but, irrationally, that she *had* to relate and that she was an utterly worthless *person*, a no-goodnik, if she didn't. She was risking her entire worth as a human, her respect for herself, on the possibility of her not relating; and naturally, with such a great stake, she was making herself inordinately anxious.

In regard to self-created anger, she was sanely telling herself, "Isn't it too bad if a man doesn't appreciate my good qualities and refuses to keep relating to me on an intimate level," and insanely telling herself, "Isn't it horrible if he doesn't appreciate my good qualities; what a turd he is for being so benighted."

To sum up: In the case of depression, she was *demanding* that she get what she wanted in the way of an intimate relationship and making herself feel hopeless and suicidal when her demands were not being met. In the case of anxiety, she was *insisting* that she succeed in relating well to every man she wanted to relate to and putting her entire self, her personhood, down when she didn't. And in the case of anger, she was *commanding* that a man in whom she was vitally interested be equally appreciative of her, and thereby hating him in toto because of his unappreciative qualities.

This, I hypothesize, is what almost invariably happens in the case of unhealthy love. Like my unrelating client, the individual dogmatically *orders* that the world conform to his love goals. By this kind of Jehovian fiat, he makes himself unusually insecure, anxious, or jealous when he *may* not be loved by someone he has selected; he induces feelings of depression, despair, hopelessness, and suicide when he *is* not adequately loved; and he frequently brings on anger, hostility, and rage at specific people who refuse to give him the love he demands.

Does superromantic idealization, which I describe in *The American Sexual Tragedy* (Ellis, 1954), which Kremen and Kremen (1971) nicely delineate, and which several other authors in this book significantly mention, also stem from the same kind of demandingness? As far as I can see, in a large part yes. For one thing, it is compensatory. For humans do not merely denigrate themselves for failing to have good love affairs, but for many other things as well: for example, failing to achieve notably in the realm of business, art, science, or social relations. When they foolishly rate themselves (instead of merely sensibly rating their traits or performances), they feel exceptionally inadequate, inferior, or rotten. Consequently, if they *could* ideally fall in love with a member of the other sex and he or she *did* gloriously love them in turn, this marvelous romantic feeling would (they imagine) at least partly perfume their shithood; and they would (at least temporarily) feel much better about themselves. So they have considerable incentives to believe that their beloved is the greatest thing since Eve and that her acceptance of them makes them the greatest thing since Adam.

There are, however, several other reasons why humans tend to idealize a member of the other sex (or in the case of homoeroticism, a member of the same sex) and to fall madly, and sometimes irrevocably, in love with someone whose qualities may be highly questionable, particularly if they are contemplating marrying this person. These other irrational reasons include:

Misperception. The beloved is actually a person with fairly ordinary traits but is misperceived as having remarkable characteristics. The lover *needs* (or thinks he needs) the beloved to be memorably intelligent, beautiful, sexy, or sincere; hence, he actually observes her to have these unpossessed features.

Fixation. The lover is treated very well by a member of the other sex (such as a father, an uncle, or a brother) during her early years and she keeps falling in love, for the rest of her days, with other members of this sex who have traits somewhat similar to those of this original person (e.g., blond hair, green eyes, or high intelligence).

Magical Identification. The lover desperately needs to be strong or goodlooking (often, because of his own feelings of inadequacy) and keeps falling in love with someone (often, a member of his own sex) who has these traits, magically believing that he will come to possess them if this other person can be induced to love him.

Narcissism. The lover really likes some of her own qualities (such as her good posture) and only becomes highly enamored of individuals with these same qualities, no matter what their other characteristics are.

Hostility. The lover hates his parents or other authority figures and consciously or unconsciously becomes infatuated with individuals who possess those features which would tend to be most offensive to the persons she hates.

Security. The lover cannot stand any form of rejection and thinks he needs to be loved totally and forever; consequently he only becomes enchanted with partners who seem to be utterly safe in this respect and will presumably adore him forever.

Romantic Illusions. The lover believes that "true love" lasts forever and only permits himself to become passionately endeared to a person who has the same romantic illusions and who swears undying devotion.

Caretaking Needs. The lover believes that she cannot stand on her own feet and that the world is too hard for her, so she becomes enormously attached to individuals who will presumably take care of her and make things easy for her for the rest of her life.

If we examine in detail these various kinds of idealized love, it can be observed that they are all forms of demandingness. The lover wants some advantages of an intimate relationship; he or she then arbitrarily and absolutistically establishes some characteristic which *must* exist if an ideal love relationship is to exist; this characteristic is then either discovered or invented in another person; and the lover usually becomes utterly convinced that the beloved (1) really possesses this exemplary characteristic; (2) will continue to possess it forever; (3) will use it for the advantage of the lover; and (4) will have a glorious ongoing relationship with the lover in spite of any other disadvantageous characteristics the beloved may possess or handicapping conditions under which the relationship will probably exist.

Because it is highly unlikely that, especially in the long run, these insistences and absolutistic predictions of the lover will be realized, the unhealthy lover almost always winds up with several kinds of disturbed feelings. For example:

Anxiety. The lover is incessantly overconcerned about whether he will find the "right" beloved, win her, and always keep her completely attached to him in the exact manner that he demands that she be attached.

Jealousy. The lover is frequently intensely jealous of the beloved, believes that he is overweeningly interested in other potential beloveds, can't stand the idea of sharing him to any extent, tends to spy on him, nag him, and paranoiacally believe that he no longer loves her and instead is devoted to someone else.

Depression. The lover thinks that his beloved does not love him sufficiently or at all; that she never will; that no one whom he wants to love him intensely ever will; that this is a horrible state of affairs; and that he will be able to obtain practically no joy in life from any source unless he is truly beloved by some enchanting person whom he loves.

Inertia. The lover is convinced that it is too hard for her to get what she wants in a love affair, that it shouldn't be this hard, and that she might as well give up and do nothing about trying to arrange and develop the kind of an affair that she thinks she has to have.

Hostility. The lover thinks that it is terribly unfair that he is not loved the way he should be loved by the person he selects, and it is horrible that this kind of injustice exists, that the individual who doesn't

love him ought to do so, and that this person is therefore a blackguard for being so unfair to him.
Worthlessness. The lover imagines that she is unloved by the person she selects because she has some exceptionally rotten traits and that therefore she is a totally rotten person who doesn't deserve to be loved by anyone.
Erotomania. Occasionally, the lover obtains considerable evidence that the person he loves does not care for him, and even detests him, but he refuses to accept this evidence and convinces himself that this person really does care, and perhaps is even madly in love with him.

Assuming that unhealthy love, or the dire need to relate intimately to another person, usually stems from dogmatic demandingness or absolutistic insistence that the world be the way the lover wants it to be, and assuming that it is a distinct pattern of emotional disturbance that often includes strong elements of anxiety, depression, worthlessness, and hostility, what can be done to ameliorate this condition? An answer, though not necessarily the complete or only answer, is intensive psychotherapy. This may take, in my estimation, two major forms: palliative or curative methods. Unfortunately, most therapy today is of the former variety, and it largely consists of the following submethods:
Love Substitution. The therapist relates warmly to the unloved and depressed client and gives him or her substitute love. The basic message conveyed to the client is: "So-and-so doesn't care for you, and never may: but *I* care. Therefore, you are really a worth-

while individual, instead of the shit you think you are, and you will always find other good people to love you." Limitations of this method: The client is confirmed in his irrational belief that he *does* need love to be a worthwhile person; and now that he is receiving it from the therapist he *is* O.K. He is not helped to change his basic demandingness, and will probably fall on his face later, when he selects another potential beloved and discovers that he or she doesn't really care for him.

Ego-bolstering. The therapist shows the client that although she may fail at winning A's love, she has the ability to win B, C, or D; and that she also can do other things well—such as a job or artistic endeavor. Consequently, the idea is conveyed that she is not a worm. Limitations: The client is never disabused of the notion that she *must* succeed at *something* in order to accept herself and enjoy her existence. She continues to remain dependent on success in order to feel worthwhile, and she retains underlying anxiety that she will fail at significant endeavors in the future.

Catharsis and Abreaction. The therapist encourages the client to ventilate his feelings, particularly his feelings of self-pity and anger. Limitations: Although some clients momentarily *feel* a lot better when using this method, they rarely *get* better. On the contrary, they more frequently than not keep believing that it *is* awful that they are not inordinately loved and that the person who rejects their love *is* a rotten individual. Their self-pity and anger,

190

at best, only temporarily abate while their disturbance-creating *philosophy* remains.

Diversion. The therapist provides various diversionary techniques, either during or outside the therapeutic sessions. These can include relaxation, massage, meditation, yoga exercises, sensory awareness training, artistic pursuits, intellectual discussion, and a large number of other diversions. Limitations: Such techniques can easily induce the client, for the nonce, to focus on more enjoyable and constructive pursuits than she has been previously concentrating on; and she may temporarily forget her dire love needs. Most of the time, however, the diversions do not permanently counterattack her basic demandingness.

Desensitizing. The therapist may desensitize the client about, say, his anxiety regarding a beloved's rejecting him or regarding his phobia about approaching a potential beloved who might refuse him. Limitations: Desensitization, unless it is accompanied by cognitive generalization, tends to work only in regard to rejection by a particular person or in regard to a phobia about a special kind of amative risk-taking. To become generally effective, the client may have to be desensitized many times in connection with several different love anxieties or phobias.

Operant Conditioning. The therapist may use reinforcements or aversive penalties to help the client love a suitable person or stop loving an unsuitable one. Limitations: This kind of therapy again tends to be overly specific instead of deconditioning the

191

client's general demanding tendencies, which he can easily transfer to another beloved.

In addition to these palliative or inelegant methods of therapy, there exist a number of curative or more elegant methods. These are concerned with making the client aware that he is an arrant demander, showing him why this philosophic outlook just will not be effective in helping him get what he wants and avoid what he does not want, and persuading, educating, and training him to give up his basic commandingness and to work for those goals he strongly *desires* rather than those he thinks he absolutely *needs*. In rational-emotive therapy (RET), in particular, some of the more elegant methods that are regularly employed include the following:

Anti-demandingness. The therapist shows the client, in accordance with the A-B-C theory of symptom-creation outlined previously in this article, that his emotional disturbance is not created by the influence of external situations or Activating Events (A) but from his own Belief system (B) and particularly from his irrational Beliefs that he *should*, *ought*, and *must* achieve the love goals that he desires. The client is also shown how to analyze, attack, ameliorate, and extirpate these irrational Beliefs by logico-empirically Disputing them (at point D).

Unconditional Positive Regard. The therapist shows the client that he has unconditional positive regard for him; that he can accept the client no matter *what* he does or how he fails. Moreover (and often more importantly) the therapist shows him how he can give himself unconditional positive regard or self-

192

acceptance: that is, by *always* refraining from rating his *self*, his *being* while still rating his *deeds*, *traits*, and *acts*. He teaches the client, by word and example, tolerance of himself and others.

Higher Frustration Tolerance. The therapist indicates to the client how he can raise his frustration tolerance; thus he helps the client convince himself that he doesn't *need* what he *wants*; that he can *stand* losses and rejections even though he'll never *like* them; that frustration may be *annoying* and *irritating* but that it's never *awful*, *horrible*, or *catastrophic*.

Emotional Education. The therapist, in order to show the client how to be tolerant of himself, others, and the difficulties of the universe, and how to stop childishly demanding that his desires be immediately gratified, uses a variety of dramatic-evocative approaches such as roleplaying, assertion training, authentic self-disclosure, and various kinds of encountering-relating methods. He uses these techniques, however, not as ends in themselves but as means of philosophic restructuring, or of revealing to the client what his self-defeating values are and how he or she can change them.

Behavior Therapy Methods. The therapist who uses the rational-emotive approach almost invariably employs *in vivo* activity-oriented homework assignments. Thus, he gives graduated assignments whereby the client takes the risks of meeting, dating, and relating to potential love partners; and he assigns the client to stay with frustrating conditions (such as an affair which is going badly) in order to learn how to tolerate these conditions before he finally (rationally and determinedly rather than irrationally and enragedly) leaves them.

In many ways, then, the RET practitioner uses a combination of cognitive-emotive-behavior methods to reveal to the client what his fundamental self-destroying and antisocial philosophies are and what he can actively and precisely do to change them. His goal is to help the client maximally accept reality (even when he doesn't like it), stop whining and wailing about it, stop foolishly exacerbating it, and persist at trying to actively change it for the better. He tries to show the client how to surrender his dictatorialness, with its concomitant compulsiveness, fixation, and fetishism, and to maximize his freedom of choice and be able to fulfill his human potential for growth and happiness.

Love is one of the greatest forces and influences in human life. It can bring enormous benefits and gains. But when the individual turns it from a powerful desire into a presumed necessity, he unrealistically endangers and minimizes it. Moreover, he usually creates gratuitous anxiety, depression, inadequacy feelings, and hostility. But all is not lost. He almost always has the capacity to reverse his childish demandingness, to grow up, and to love in a nonobligatory manner. One of the main purposes of effective psychotherapy is to help him do love compellingly but uncompulsively. A difficult but hardly impossible goal.

REFERENCES

de Rougemont, D. *Love in the western world*. New York: Harcourt, Brace, 1940.

Ellis, A. A study of human love relationships. *Journal of Genetic Psychology,* 1949a, 75, 61-71.

Ellis, A. A study of the love emotions of American college girls. *International Journal of Sexology,* 1949b, 3, 15-21.

Ellis, A. Some significant correlates of love and family behavior. *Journal of Social Psychology.* 1949c, 30, 3-16.

Ellis, A. Love and family relationships of American college girls. *American Journal of Sociology,* 1950, 55, 550-558.

Ellis, A. *The American sexual tragedy*. New York: Twayne Publishers, 1954. Revised ed., New York: Lyle Stuart and Grove Press, 1962.

Ellis, A. *How to live with a neurotic*. New York: Crown Publishers, 1957. Revised ed., New York: Award Books, 1969.

Ellis, A. *Sex without guilt*. New York: Lyle Stuart, 1958. Revised ed., New York: Lyle Stuart and Lancer Books, 1969.

Ellis, A. *The art and science of love*. New York: Lyle Stuart, 1960. Revised ed., New York: Lyle Stuart and Bantam Books, 1969.

Ellis, A. *Reason and emotion in psychotherapy*. New York: Lyle Stuart, 1962.

Ellis, A. *If this be sexual heresy . . .* New York: Lyle Stuart and Tower Publications, 1963.

Ellis, A. *Growth through reason*. Palo Alto: Science and Behavior Books, 1971.

Ellis, A. *Executive leadership: A rational approach*. New York: Citadel Press, 1972.

Ellis, A., and Gullo, J. M. *Murder and assassination*. New York: Lyle Stuart, 1971.

Ellis, A., and Harper, R. A. *A guide to rational living*. Englewood Cliffs, N.J.: Prentice-Hall, 1961a; Hollywood: Wilshire Books, 1971.

Ellis, A., and Harper, R. A. *Creative marriage*. New York: Lyle Stuart, 1961b; Hollywood: Wilshire Books, 1970.

Finck, H. T. *Romantic love and personal beauty*. New York: Macmillan, 1887.

Fromm, E. *The art of loving*. New York: Harper, 1962.

Grant, V. *Psychology of sexual emotion*. New York: Longmans, Green, 1957.

Kremen, H., and Kremen, B. Romantic love and idealization. *American Journal of Psychoanalysis*, 1971, 31, 134-143.

Levy, J. and Munroe, R. *The happy family*. New York: Knopf, 1938.

Lucka, E. *Evolution of love*. London: Allen and Unwin, 1922.

Maslow, A. H. Love in healthy people. In A. Montagu (Ed.), *The meaning of love*. New York: Julian Press, 1953.

Montagu, A. (Ed.). *The meaning of love*. New York: Julian Press, 1953.

Ortega y Gasset, J. *On love*. New York: Meridian, 1960.

Reik, T. *A psychologist looks at love.* New York: Rinehart, 1945.

Salzman, L. A psychiatrist discusses falling in love. *Sexual Behavior*, 1971, 1 (1), 16-21.

Sorokin, P. A. *The ways and power of love.* Boston: Beacon, 1954.

Stendhal. *On love.* New York: Liveright, 1947.

10

The Meaning of Love in the Black Experience

Shirley W. Thomas

"love: a strong affection for or attachment
to a person or persons; a strong liking for
or interest in Something." Webster

To ANALYZE THE basic premises of the thrust of the
Black experience, one must understand some
specific areas of developing beliefs among Black
people. The values, codes of behavior, and mores
that Black people are developing (based upon beliefs
and life styles of the past, such as those ingredients
of tribal life that are found to be functional for
today's urban Black family) are directly counter to
Western cultural beliefs as they are known in this
country.

The strong affection for or attachment to a *person*
or *persons* that is fundamental to a definition of love

199

is a very basic interpretation of the meaning of building a sense of community. Community-building leads to experiences in relatedness that create a sense of self that is founded upon feeling; this is closely related to what is commonly called love. Obviously, the question of love from this frame of reference becomes broader than it is usually considered to be.

As we analyze the needs, goals, and life styles of Black people who have begun to participate in the Black experience, we see love in many forms: love of one human for another, love of man and woman, love of parent for child, love of child for parent, love of sibling for sibling. We observe a developing devotion to goals, an attachment to those who are Black or trying to become Black, and an interest in those things that must be developed in behalf of Black people.

Most of the consumers of Westernized culture become impaled on the spikes of frustration, inadequate feelings, and a negative sense of self because they have ascribed to the dysfunctional modes of Westernized love. It is these modes of behavior, stimulated and reinforced by the very nature of Western society, that destroy and will continue to destroy those Afro-Americans who attempt to emulate those values of the dominant group.

The dysfunctional modes of love for the non-Black individual are those modes that use the sense of love in a self-perpetuating, self-aggrandizing manner. That is, most Western non-Blacks use love to gain an end that is not necessarily *mutually* beneficial to those involved in the so-called love experience. In the Black experience, on the other hand, love is an encompassing life style that has within it the *mutual* well-being of those involved in the love experience.

The concept of Harambee, or "let's pull together," is seen by Blacks who are concerned about behavior change as being the manner in which those who feel disenfranchised or disengaged can become a part of a unit, from which support is gained. This support, which is actually a system of supports, serves to introduce different modes of potential behavior to the individual and to offer other life strategies for his consideration.

For social experience to be positive, there must be an interrelatedness among individuals that gives them a positive social support system. Such motivation enables them to become optimally functional, not only in behalf of themselves, but in behalf of others in the social environment. Love interrelatedness involves the mutuality of goal setting and attaining and successful resolution of negatives in the environment. When, however, the interrelatedness is disturbed by a superimposition of Western life style, then the values that those individuals are attempting to develop are less than useful to them. When the healthy, mature person chooses to remain in similar situations, it is because there is a strong need for the positive rewarding circumstances of those situations. The result is successful because the appropriate behaviors for positive interpersonal relations are in the person-social repertory. Consequently, there is self-respect, self-worth, and a sense of sharing that becomes the basis of communal behavior. If a person gets something from an involvement, he usually gives as much back as he gets. Between individuals in a relationship, there is a circular effect, that of continual renewal that serves as a revitalizing process.

In the Black experience, the above notion is expanded to encompass not only two individuals, but other-sized social units as well: the smaller unit is the Black family; the median unit is the community, and the larger unit is that social environment (society) in which individuals reside and/or navigate through. It implies providing the arena for re-birth of both ideas and goals. The shared relationships serve as vehicles for encouraging deep involvement and commitment to others as a means of enhancement of self.

When Black people speak of developing a sense of community, generally this means that positive experiences with each other are repeated again and again, and extended to include those who may not be experiencing that which could be positive for them. When defeating or destructive situations have to be dealt with, this extension of self into that sphere of other individuals then provides a support system that has within it strategies for analysis of the problem and its resolution in a mutually beneficial manner.

Mutuality of thrust and concern is fundamentally developed from Black experiences as multifaceted modes of behaviors that we utilize to develop ourselves and aid in the development of those around us in the primary environment, i.e., the environment that directly affects our lives. When goals are set mutually, those involved in the goal setting assume the responsibility of developing strategies to attain those goals. This process also makes possible the development of strategies by others in the goal-setting process who may not be totally involved in the Black experience but are attempting to become so.

Love, then, is seen as an enabling experience; one that forms the basis for involvement in Black affairs, or affairs affecting Black people. The basis for behavior in this instance is that of continual motivation so that one can engage in the processes that affect one's life, and in doing so bring about more positive change. To better understand what is being indicated here, the following components must be kept in mind. Primarily, love in the Black experience is based upon a mutuality of thrust, and the concept of love extends beyond that which is usually considered in Western society: sexual and physical relations or material acquisition. Thus, love in the Black experience encompasses the refining of a socially productive value system and emphasizes extension of oneself and interactive behavior—"I am the Black community, the Black community is me."

There are many instances in which one may be in the process of extending oneself. For our purposes here, let us consider four basic extensions: Black man to Black woman, Black woman to Black man, parents to family, and family to community.

The relationships between Black men and Black

women must go through refinements on a continual basis, because as the demands of Blackness develop, Black men and women must ascertain those modes of behavior which will be of greatest value to them. The Black man has to go through the process of being and becoming so that he can then transmit to his woman his ability to define the role he wishes to assume, not only with her but also with those he will be interacting with. The Black man must decide for himself who he wants to be, how he wants to achieve who he wants to be, and then extend himself beyond himself in order to affect those around him.

In relating to the Black woman, the Black man begins to experience a sense of worth, a diminishment of frustration, and a regard for the woman that places her in the position of being the recipient of positive inputs. Once the Black man begins engaging in activities that he is suited for, that he has chosen, he is then able to create an environment in which love can flourish. But the love that does flourish is not traditional romantic love; it is rather a love that encompasses a pure sense of fulfillment which stems from being with people one wishes to be with, in situations one wishes to be in, and in places where one wishes to go. The value of extending oneself in the Black experience relates to what I like to designate as the "thinking Black, feeling Black, being Black" orientation. One is truly engaging in the Black experience if one does not engage in strategies of destruction directed against those who are sharing any arc of one's circle of involvement in the Black communion.

The Black woman, in relating to the Black man, must determine whether she can comfortably assume a role that is very different from the one she has been accustomed to. She should cease viewing the male as an insensitive, inept, insecure person and should begin to perceive him as possessing the positive opposites of the above. To do so, she must utilize the frame of reference of the Black experience and not of the dominant society. Role definitions, modes of behavior, and value sets must be devised according to what is seen as functional to and for the Black male and female.

In order to enhance her chosen mode of behavior, the Black woman learns to determine the quality and amount of inputs she allows into her personal sphere. She then begins to develop her relationship with her man in a manner that is conducive to a positive growth relationship between the two. One of the problems, however, is creating a strong enough buffer zone, so to speak, between the Black couple and the bombardment tendencies of the outer environment. The strategies that need to be developed take on the characteristics of what may be termed counter-bombardment; that is, for every negative element that attempts to invade the environment, a positive block must be thrown up.

I will not deal with historical points of view here, except to say that the Black woman in contemporary society sees herself in concert with, not in conflict with, her man; she learns to be an image builder, not an image destroyer; and she has an influence on young Black people which supports the notions of youth, giftedness, and Blackness. This, then, is a form of Black love.

For too long, the Black family has been perceived in a negative, dysfunctional manner. It is, then, the task of Black parents to create, within the sphere of the family, a life style that serves to counteract as much as possible the destructive forces affecting the Black family in today's society. The Black male in the family unit serves as a provider of resources both physical and emotional; the Black female in the unit acts as a supportive agent as well as one who transmits to the family those values that are deemed necessary for the growth and survival of the family.

Many of today's Black people find themselves wondering if what they are doing and trying to do will enable them to determine the course of their lives in a more effective manner than in the past. It is therefore important that they assume the attitude that the primary goal is the movement of Black people from mere survival to a more growth-oriented and rewarding existence. Love, then, encompasses those facets of daily existence that enable an individual to be what he wants to be, to do what he feels he wants to do, and to say what he wants to say.

In extending the family to the community, three

206

concepts must be ever-present: concern, commitment, and accountability. When the Black family
engages in activities in the community, the underlying premise is that one is involved because of love.
The Black teacher transmitting knowledge effec-
tively is showing Black love; the professionals who
share their skills and knowledge are exhibiting love;
the community worker who disseminates factual
information to the masses is doing so in the name
of Black love; the individual, who attempts to change
or modify social systems so that they serve people
better is doing so because of love. The individual
who has had no experiences that are rewarding and
fulfilling and who engages in behavior that is
destructive to himself and others is allowing himself
to function in the realm of the "negro" syndrome.
That is, he is doing those things that are of no value
to himself or his people.

Blackness can definitely be the elixir that produces
love in many forms. What each individual does,
thinks, and feels affects everyone who comes in contact with him. Moreover, the concept of the Black
experience as a positive mode of behavior induces
mental healthiness in those individuals in pursuit of
a more satisfying life style.

"I am the Black community, the Black community
is me" is the concept that can enable individuals to
move into various arenas in a manner that is instruc-
tive rather than destructive. The psycho-social
aspects of the *I* of an individual should lead him to

the *we* of an experience. However, when the *me* is the community there can be no *I*. Continual interaction between members of the Black community leads to predictability of behavior which then increases the positive aspects of relationships. For example, when individuals come together to solve what is considered to be a communal problem (an instance such as the condition of the public schools), they begin to reflect upon each other's approach to problem solving; and over a period of time they learn to differentiate and reject those strategies that are not functional for the situation and begin to effect more functional substitute strategies. When mutuality of thrust is the basis for action, those involved can begin to celebrate the validity of differences in a positively-oriented, developmental manner. Commitment to the notion that love encompasses many areas of feeling and involvement enables those in the process of experiencing Blackness to give priority to those activities that enhance themselves and the community.

To be Black in the last half of the twentieth century requires a redefinition and redirection of all that has a negative impact on Black people. The importance of the new notion of what constitutes love in the Black experience cannot be over-emphasized. The dominant society places many barriers, both seen and unseen, before us, and the functions of these barriers are to diminish us, deter us, define us, and direct us in such a manner that we will find it exceedingly difficult to develop a style of living that is congruent with our notion of Blackness.

The meaning of love in the Black experience is

simply this: we allow no one to diminish us as Black human beings; we allow no one to diminish our families as positive Black families; we allow no diminishment of our communities as progressive Black communities; and we allow no further diminishment of our world into a nonliberated one.

11

Love and Respect

Edith Weigert

THE WORD "love" has many definitions and meanings. Love seems to me to be an aim of human yearn-
ings, but it is not an accomplishment, neither in the
child nor in the mature adult. Love is not a thing
and I do not think it can be considered pathological;
and here my views, then, differ from those stated
earlier by Dr. Casler. Freedom is another aim of
human longing. Scientists call it an illusion, since it
is unreachable; yet is it a universal illusion and men
have sacrificed their lives for it. Also, Truth is not
an accomplishment; the truth of yesterday can
become error tomorrow; but the yearning and striving is therewith not extinguished. The German poet
Lessing expressed an opinion concerning truth
which I can only paraphrase from memory: "If God
held in His right hand truth and in His left hand
the striving for truth, I would grasp His left hand,

for truth is in God alone, not accessible to man."
The same holds true when the Bible says "God is
Love." An atheist would say that truth, freedom,
and love belong in the realm of ideals and aims
that cannot even be approximated by human beings,
yet they exist powerfully in human yearning and
striving throughout man's development. Even before
a child can verbalize or conceptualize the yearning for love, freedon, and truthfulness, he expresses his emotional protest against deprivation of
love and restraint of freedom in movement and self-
expression; and he senses the truthfulness in genuine
care for his well-being. The yearning for these
values must be innate.

The American psychiatrist Harry Stack Sullivan
(1940) and the German philosopher Martin Heidegger (1962) defined love as man's care for his fellow
man as he cares for himself. But human care that
results in mere survival is far from perfection. Man's
care for others as well as for himself is frequently
less successful than mutual care in the animal kingdom. In a beehive or an anthill, we see an excellent
social organization, where every individual instinc-
tively fulfills his function in harmony with the
cooperative organization of the total group. Animal
society is not torn by wars and revolutions. Konrad
Lorenz (1963), the ethologist, has shown that in most
animal species there is a built-in instinct-barrier
against damaging the life of a fellow member of the
species. When a combat for leadership breaks out in
a pack of wolves, two rivals may fight until one's
superiority in strength has been demonstrated; the

vanquished wolf then offers his jugular vein to the victor to bite, but the victor does not bite. Thus the Latin proverb *homo homoni lupus* does not fit any more, since man's behavior is frequently not so merciful as the described behavior of wolves.

Mephistopheles, the devil in Goethe's *Faust*, complains to God the Lord, "Why did you give to man the divine light of reason? He only uses his reasoning power to behave more beastly than the beasts." The frustrations that arise from imperfections in the adjustment of man to man, of man to woman and woman to man, of older to younger, etc., are far from the perfection that human beings are longing for. Man's imagination has fought this frustration with ideals expressed in primitive mythologies and more philosophically oriented religions, but even the Christian Gospel of love was unable to prevent the Crusades and other cruel persecution of opponents of the established dogma. The French Revolution abolished the suprahuman deity and replaced Him with the human potentiality of reasoning; but the ideals of justice, equality, and brotherly love in human societies have not reached a higher degree of realization under the rule of human reasoning power.

In distinction from animals, human freedom of choice, though limited, is enlarged by man's consciousness and foresight. But freedom of choice is closely related to fear and anxiety. Fear and anxiety frequently counteract the bond of sympathy, the integrative principle that holds men together in the smaller and larger communities of families, societies, and nations. The French existentialist, Jean-Paul Sartre (1948), sees, within the context of the struggle for existence, the individual longing for freedom as a force that inhibits the instinct of sympathy, the yearning for love. The individual striving for the freedom to pursue his own happiness, to guarantee gratification and security for himself and his fellows, has achieved miracles of mastery over the material world due to the expansion of science and technology; but man cannot manipulate other men as if they were matter without arousing fears and anxieties. According to Sartre, man tends to strive for his own freedom to pursue happiness at the expense of his fellows' freedom. "Remove yourself so that I can take your place"—this notion rules in unbridled competition and creates sado-masochistic interactions and relations that contradict the spirit of love and the ideal of freedom. It arouses the fear of men in man. To appease these fears and their repercussions of defiance, anger, rage, destructiveness, and vindictiveness, man pretends to care for his fellow men, to love where he really fears, to serve where he really dominates, to bribe in order to exploit. These false pretenses, these defenses against the painful experiences of anxieties in the relationships of man to man, of man to woman, or of woman to man are designated by Sartre as demonstrations of "bad faith." They are not necessarily psychopathological symptoms. They pervade the social life of every day existence in the hypocrisies of adaptation to conventionality. The mask of fitting in, belonging—as far as it is primarily dictated by the

214

anxiety of being deserted as an unwanted outsider, ostracized, excommunicated—degrades the authenticity, the spontaneity, and the genuineness of the human being. This mask is called by Heidegger "man," the German impersonal pronoun, meaning everybody, the so-called normal person that does not exist. Heidegger postulated that only the individual who is able to face death can be authentic, truly himself. It is true that behind any deprivation, any frustration, any loss of gratifications and security there lurks the unconscious fear of death, which implies loneliness, helplessness, and powerlessness.

Tolerance of frustration exists in different degrees in various individuals and in different episodes of the life span. Frustration tolerance is lowest in the infant who is helpless, more helpless than any new-born animal; his needs are simple, yet not verbalized in the beginning. The sympathetic intuition of the responsible adults respects the child's growing potentialities of mastery and self-sufficiency as well as his relative helplessness. Adults take care of the child's needs, protect him from unmanageable dangers, and set limits to his expansive aggression, expressed by the impulsive, childish insistence, "I want what I want, when I want it." Parents are frequently not able to manage their own frustrations. In that case they frequently misuse the helpless child for their own gratification or they abandon the child emotionally, since he or she is an imposition on their own freedom to pursue happiness. Either neglect or excessive indulgence hampers the development of frustration tolerance and the adequate growth of

215

mastery and self-sufficiency. The individual with low frustration tolerance is oversensitized by anxieties; the world appears to him to be a dismal place; people are envied enemies that cannot be trusted; the unconscious fear of annihilation (inevitable death) overshadows consciousness, bursting out in nightmares or temper tantrums. The yearning for love is intensified under these conditions, but it has to be repressed out of fear of more frustrations and punitive repercussions. Hope may turn into despair; yet we also observe in such people spontaneous recovery from defeat and the development of alternative forms of conflict solution that open up new channels of development.

Sigmund Freud (1953) originally saw the sexual instincts in rebellion against the demands of self-preservation and reasonable self-assertion. In the earliest period, he described oral greed, and later anal defiance, oedipal exclusive possessiveness and sticky dependency, destructive sibling rivalry, penis envy, and castration anxieties. These rebellious instincts were not only dictated by libidinal, pregenital, and genital urges, but also by generalized fear of frustration of all vital needs, by anxiety about individual survival, by fear of death more than trust in life.

In his later writings, Freud extended the sexual instinct to Eros, the Life Instinct. His friend Ludwig Binswanger (1953) called this life instinct *Eros heauton auxon*, which means the self-increasing, ever-expanding love of life. Freud's contemporaries, the philosopher Henri Bergson (1944) and the French psychiatrist Eugene Minkowski (1970), saw in the life instinct the *élan vital*, a spiritual force, the integrative principle that transcends anxieties and reconciles conflicts of ambivalence. According to the French authors, the *élan vital* functions in rhythmic waves of stimulation and relaxation, swinging from exuberance to exhaustion, ultimately succumbing to the final destiny of life, the unpredictable, inevitable, but ever threatening destiny of mortality. Due to his spiritual endowment, man can transcend in creative sublimations the fear of death, the futile protest against the separations, losses, and frustrations of human existence. A creative composer, Johann Sebastian Bach, sang in jubilant gratitude, "Ich freue mich auf meinen Tod," (I rejoice looking forward to my death) and "Ich habe genug," (I have enough).

Freud was not inclined to see in the acceptance of death a spiritual achievement of reconciling sublimation. He refused to leave the biological basis of his instinct theory and the dialectical conflicts of biological drives. He saw the low voice of reason as the only support for an advance from the pleasure-pain principle to the reality principle of adaption. Ernest Jones (1955) describes Freud's deep disappointment when his favorite disciple, C. G. Jung, left the exclusively biological basis of their psychoanalytic studies and emphasized the spiritual potentialities of unifying the constructive and destructive tendencies in vital impulses.

Freud maintained the tragic conflict of contradictory biological instincts: sexual instinct versus self-preservation, narcissistic versus object libido, i.e.,

217

self-love versus love of others. In his later essay *Beyond the Pleasure Principle* (1955), he opposed Eros, the life instinct, and Thanatos, the death instinct, the biological source of aggression. Freud's concept of instinct was different from that of biologists and ethologists. It was admittedly a mythological concept. A number of Freud's disciples had reservations concerning the notion of a death instinct. But Freud made us think about how much death prevades life from start to finish. While Eros, the life instinct, rushes to new discoveries, new risks, broadening conquests, and possible defeats, the death instinct seems to aim at security and peace in the turbulent struggle for survival. Sleep, the brother of death, provides relaxation in the struggle for gratifications and security. Dreams, in their disorganization, present the magical conflict solutions of man's private imagination. New energies are gathered in the withdrawal into the privacy of sleep. The orgasm that the French call *la petite mort* relaxes the tensions of sexual urges. The automatisms of habits relieve man of the challenge of decision-making. They may freeze into self-centered defenses. But the repetition compulsion, the phenomenon of transference, brings up traumatic past experience in a present situation for revisions and possible new solutions. Anxiety is the warning signal that stirs man up in his longing for rest, peace, and harmony. Anxiety escalated into panic might freeze man into a torpor of boring inactivity; in ultimate extremes, panic elicits a catatonic stupor, a living death, or it arouses a protest-storm of impotent rage which cannot arrive at conflict solutions.

The aggressive instinct is only a servant of death when it, unbridled and untamed, insists on magic removal of all dangers, all enemies. It stems from the need for security, but it leads ultimately to disorganization and disintegration. The tamed aggressive impulse, on the other hand, can create novelties of conflict solution and integration in the service of life.

It is hard for human beings to reach an harmonious integration of the need for gratifications and the longing for security by a balance of love and respect, respect for one's own needs as well as for the needs of one's companion in interpersonal relations. The difficulty in reaching such a balance is largely due to the long period of relative helplessness of the child and his dependency on the security of the family. The discrepancy of power between parents and children is a temptation for the parents to exploit the child for their own gratification, to direct him by overprotection, or to expose him to conflicting influences. The child is tempted to make the parents feel guilty and to manipulate them into excessive gratifications by pleasing them or intimidating them by temper tantrums or defiance reactions.

At the time of puberty, the urge for sexual gratifications becomes intense along with the yearning for independence and freedom from authority, but the youngster at the age of puberty is not yet ready to take care of his needs, not yet able to hold a job or prepare for professional training without parental support. He or she is not in the least ready to pro-create children and take care of a family. If he or she is reasonably prepared to use birth control, the young adolescents, timidly or daringly, dive into their early sexual experiences. Competition is frightening, rejections are discouraging. Youngsters cling all the more to the ideal of love when they are disillusioned about their idealization of parental love and threatened by sibling rivalry. Reaching the joy of a mutual orgasm in a heterosexual union is an intensely reassuring, uplifting experience, but it is not a guarantee for a durable relationship of mutual respect and responsibility. Respect carries the ring of authoritarian supremacy. It therefore threatens the adolescent who is striving for freedom and independence. Early heterosexual experiments are loaded with anxieties, fears of failures in the performance of the sexual act, doubts regarding the choice of partner, timidities, and inhibitions ingrained by a merely-prohibitive sex education. All these anxieties elicit a wide variety of defense reac-tions. Egocentric concern dampens the development of spontaneous emotions. The male adolescent may want to prove his male prowess, the female her irresistibility. Such egocentric, defensive attitudes lower respect and mutual consideration. One partner may feel exploited when he or she has to continually lift the partner's self-esteem. The sexual activity may deteriorate into an indoor sport. Other adolescents overcompensate for their anxieties by the idealizations of romantic love. The male becomes

Prince Charming in the imagination of the female, and she the adorable fairy princess who will fulfill all his longing and yearning. These ideals of perfection lead to some disillusionment when the romantic infatuation, sooner or later, leads to a commitment and to the tests of living together in the close intimacy of daily companionship.

Daily companionship is a challenge and demands sacrifices of both partners. A person may be willing to be crucified for mankind, but cannot stand to share the bedroom with a snoring partner. A legend of the Middle Ages tells about a German community, Weinsberg, which was beleaguered and defeated by enemy forces. The enemy demanded that all men of this community be killed, but the women with children could leave unmolested and could carry with them on their back their most precious possession. All the women left the beleaguered fortress carrying their husbands on their backs. Some centuries later, a man had written on his tombstone: "My wife has not carried me like the faithful wives of Weinsberg, but she has endured me year in, year out, that was a greater burden than I can express in words."

This endurance test, endurance of both partners, confronts men and women when the idealization of romantic love fades away. There are cultures where the courtship of romantic love is avoided. The choice of marital partners is not in the hands of adolescents, but is determined by the deliberations of older, responsible family members. I do not know whether this custom facilitates more harmonious

221

marriages or lowers the divorce rate. In any case, young men and women in our culture have the freedom of choice, and wedding ceremonies are loaded with jubilant, idealistic expectations.

We hear the hippies sing: "Love, not war." This is the yearning for salvation from strife, for peace. It is the yearning for love of all mankind; but love is never without the fear of death. In every loss, in every frustration, we are confronted with ultimate death. It takes courage to open yourself up to love, taking the risk of disappointment, frustration, loss, and death. Love cannot be forced, as you would build a house from inorganic material for your gratification and security. The freedom to pursue happiness of one partner may interfere with the freedom of the other partner. Example: A husband returns from a business trip with jubilant joy. "I had an ecstatic love affair." He does not yet intend to leave wife and children, but why does he brag about the affair? Why must he tell her? He is proud of his freedom from conventionality, but does he express self-centered guilt feelings about his infidelity? His wife is hurt. She has another idea of freedom to pursue happiness. She finds greater freedom in the security of the home than in the transient gratifications of orgastic pleasure. She feels threatened and forced to make a decision. Shall she swallow her pride, submit in estrangement, or leave in distress, or threaten to leave in order to force him into submission? Their ideals of freedom are incompatible. Arguments do not solve the conflict. There is no right or wrong. There is not a sufficient bond of sympathy, or even tact, dictated by respect for the partner's needs. They do not understand each other's need for freedom. Is marriage an outmoded institution? Is commitment a prison? And what about the children? They long for security even more than the wife. They still need the idealization of parental love. It is freqently better to end the warfare of the parents by separation than to expose the children to having to take sides in the parents' sado-masochistic involvements. Good nurses are not always available. Day care centers can be useful, but not always adequate. Institutionalized upbringing has all the disadvantages of impersonal distance which denies to the child the needed closeness of security. One child who was brought up in an orphanage with infrequent maternal visits became an adult who could not commit himself to a stable relationship: he wandered from one affair to another, searching for the ideal mate who would make up for the frustrations of his childhood.

The human child is so helpless in comparison to the adult's strength and intelligence that only the bond of intuitive empathy finds the right balance between closeness and distance, dependency and growing independence, protection and freedom. Intuitive empathy cannot be quantitatively measured and prescribed. It is not only dictated by love but also by respect because love without respect for the weaker partner can be overpowering and can squelch the freedom to develop, or else the stronger partner feels overpowered by the weaker partner's unlimited demands; this is the omnipotent wishful

223

denial of the weaker partner's relative helplessness. When a young mother after the delivery succumbs to a post-partum depression, she frequently is over-whelmed by the challenges of maternal care. She may feel imprisioned by her commitment. 'She has not yet found the balance of love and respect, respect for her child as well as for herself.

Any intimate relationship is based on the balance of love and respect. Love is not enough (Bettelheim, 1950). Respect is partially dictated by realistic fears, by responsibilities for the partner's life and freedom, and by fear of the curtailment of one's own vital needs by the commitment to the partner. Failures in finding the balance are often accompanied by guilt feelings and a degeneration of responsibility. Responsibility considers both the limited freedom of the partners as well as the limited freedom of one's own development. Guilt throws the individual back on himself, on his self-accusations or his self-pity; this is accompanied by magical atonement gestures. Guilt results in alienation from love and respect. Guilt is elicited by a super-ego that is not integrated into the individual's identity; it weakens the strength of the ego. Guilt makes a person dependent on fears of external authority, public disapproval, ostracism, and helplessness. The child and the adult whose ego remains weak are overly susceptible to the emotions of the partner. Excessive empathy paralyzes self-respect; the helper becomes helpless; cooperation breaks down; the bond of sympathy degenerates into contempt or excessive adulation.

The word respect is closely related to responsibility which respects or responds to the needs of the partner, but which also looks forward and grasps the partner's developmental potentialities and limitations. Dependency on immediate instinctual gratification of the aggressive or the sexual drive cannot do justice to the balance of love and respect which depends on a successsful process of integration and sublimation. The instincts are not only desexualized and deaggressivized; they are rechannelized towards novel aims, more creative than defensive aims.

The human being, not only the child, is helpless without the cooperation of his fellow men. This cooperation, which is guaranteed in the animal kingdom by innate automatic instincts, is supported by man's reasoning power, but the intellect is not enough. The egocentric defenses against fears and anxieties seduce man into phantasies of being limitlessly identical with his aims: he becomes allpowerful, all-loving and lovable, divine in his freedom and possession of truth. These Promethean defenses are tamed by what Albert Schweitzer (1949) called the reverence of life, a bond of sympathy that honors even the adversary who interferes with the immediate gratification of one's needs. The capacity to wait, to postpone, to modify wishes, to reconcile conflicts, to endure the contradictions of love and hate and of life and death stems from an innate reverence for what there is, in contrast to what there could be or should be. The reverence of life, inseparable from death, is the basis of self-respect; and if this self-respect is not corrupted by excessive wishes or excessive anxieties, it naturally produces the respect of others, opens avenues of development, and sets limits to overreaching demands.

The German word for respect is *Ehrfurcht*—honoring fear. Martin Luther introduced the explanations of the Ten Commandments with a recommendation to love and fear God in order to be able to live up to each commandment. Rudolf Otto (1932), in his book on sanctity (*Das Heilige*), describes the religious emotions associated with the Godhead, the Mysterium Tremendum, which inspire fascination and fear. In religion as well as in art, man finds compensation for his unfulfilled wishes and alleviation of his anxieties. But the creativity of art and religion can be corrupted by man's egocentricity, his excessive need to be gratified and protected. These needs produce superstitions, intolerance, and fanaticism against all who do not share particular beliefs. The dependency on religion does not always reach the level of true sublimations.

I have tried to show how the relations of man to man, man to woman, and woman to man inspire love and fear; fear of the imminent danger of loss, and the more remote danger of death, as well as fear of the challenges and responsibilities of life. The integration of love and fear (devotion and mutual respect for the I and the Thou [Buber, 1952]) expressed in the honest spontaneous encounter of two partners does not create perfect interpersonal relations or everlasting harmony and peace, but it does lead to the optimum of creative collaboration that human beings can reach.

226

REFERENCES

Bergson, H. *Creative evolution.* Translated by A. Mitchell. New York: The Modern Library, Random House, 1944.

Bettelheim, B. *Love is not enough.* New York: The Free Press, 1950.

Binswanger, L. *Grundformen und Erkenntnis Menschlichen Daseins.* Zürich: Max Niehans Verlag, 1953.

Buber, M. *I and thou.* Translated by R. G. Smith. Edinburgh: T. & T. Clark, 1952.

Freud, S. *Three essays on sexuality.* Standard Edition Vol. VII. London: The Hogarth Press, 1953, pp. 135-230.

Freud, S. *Beyond the pleasure principle.* Standard Edition Vol. XVIII. London: The Hogarth Press, 1955, pp. 7-61.

Heidegger, M. *Being and time.* A translation of *Sein und Zeit* by J. Macquarrie and E. Robinson. New York: Harper and Row, 1962.

Jones, E. *The life and work of Sigmund Freud.* New York: Basic Books, Inc., 1955, Vol. 2, pp. 137-147.

Lorenz, K. *Das sogenannte Boese.* Wien: Dr. G. Borotha-Schoeller Verlag, 1963, p. 198.

Minkowski, E. *Lived time.* Phenomenological Studies. Translated by N. Metzel. Evanston: North-Western University Press, 1970.

Otto, R. *Das Heilige.* Müenchen: C. H. Becksche Verlagsbuchhandlung, 1932.

Sartre, J. P. *L'Etre et le néant.* Paris: Libraire Gallimard, 1948.

Schweitzer, A. *Out of my life and thought: An autobiography.* Translated by C. T. Campion. The New American Library, Henry Holt, 1949.

Sullivan, H. S. Conceptions of modern psychiatry. Reprinted from *Psychiatry*, Vol. 3, No. 1, Feb. 1940, p. 20.

12

A Lovers' Post-Symposium Dialogue

Lewis R. Lieberman

AFTER THE SYMPOSIUM was over, I got caught in the crush of the audience leaving the meeting room and happened to be right behind a couple of starry-eyed kids. I couldn't help overhearing their comments on the symposium. And then I followed them for as long as I could without seeming too obvious. Here, reconstructed from my notes, is what I overheard:

HE: Well, you know, the word "symposium" originally meant drinking party. Do you feel like you've just been to a drinking party?

SHE: I don't know about the party bit, but I sure feel drowsy.

HE: I know what you mean; all that analysis and theorizing is heavy stuff.

SHE: Yeah, but more than that. I have the feeling that somehow all that technical jargon is inappropriate to the subject. Love is something to sing about, to rhapsodize about, to experience, to live. When you start getting abstract about it, it begins to seem like you're talking about something else.

HE: It loses something in the translation.

SHE: Like my feeling for you, darling, gives me a kind of joy, a glow. It makes everything seem different. To me it's something almost palpable. It's not abstract—its not what *they* were talking about.

HE (singing): But your feeling for me, baby, is just institutionalized ir-ra-tion-al-i-ty.

SHE: That's a kind of spooky idea. I feel that my love is unique, that our relationship is just ours; and yet I feel it is also something I share with other people, all other people.

HE (very professional sounding): But don't you realize that you are just exhibiting a cultural pattern? There are societies that don't even have any love.

SHE: That's too glib. It's like saying that after all, Shakespeare's plays are just funny black squiggles on a piece of paper. But the one who frightened me more was the other guy who talked about love being just dependency and breeding resentment. I believe he defined love as the fear of losing an important source of gratification.

HE: But it doesn't feel that way. Love doesn't *feel* like fear. You don't *feel* that way, do you?

SHE: No, not now. But you look around you and you see others, older people, getting divorces. Or you meet people who are married but seem to be staying together instead of living together. And even if there weren't the others, you just know that if you fell *into* love, you might fall out. And *that's* frightening. I don't feel that I *chose* to love you; therefore, even though I don't choose it, I may wake up one day and not love you any more.

HE: I can't believe it could happen to us.

SHE: Love contains the seed of its own destruction. Would you love me if I stopped loving you? Would I love you, if you stopped loving me?

HE: I don't know. I guess if you stopped loving me and wanted out and I still loved you, I'd let you go—I'd have to. Maybe it's when both stop loving that they cling to each other. It's hard to analyze; I guess I'd make a lousy social scientist.

SHE: It's just hard to answer when you're in love. I guess that's why they didn't have any lovers on the panel.

HE: Wait a minute. You remember that book we read, by Erich Fromm, *The Art of Loving*?

SHE: Yeah. You thought it was a sex manual.

HE: Well, he says in there that true loving is an *activity*—sharing and caring—between mature people.

SHE: Who do you know that's mature?

HE: That's not the point. He talks about immature love as being a symbiotic kind of relation. That's what the love-fear guy was talking about, and maybe what one of the other guys called "pregenital love."

SHE: One of them called it "unhealthy love."

HE: For Fromm, this kind of love is under the sway of passion; it's a reaction. Mature love is freely given: it is an action, not a reaction.

SHE: Then this true love is not an emotion, it is

not something that happens to you, it is something *you* make happen. But that makes it sound like any two of these mature people could be paired up at random and make it work. I don't experience my love for you that way. I care and I give and I feel like I give freely, not for return. But I do it *because* I love you. I want to do it for *you*; I don't feel that I'd like to do it for just any old mature person, buddy.

HE: Then it's a dilemma. If love is an act of will, you can will to love forever, you can't fall out of it, but then the object of this act can be anybody. If love is based on a strong feeling, a passion, then it can be directed only to the source of this passion; but it runs the risk of dying—the feeling may burn itself out.

SHE: In the first case, you have the commitment and with it security. In the other case, you give up security in return for the excitement, the joy of passion.

HE: There *could* be joy in love-by-commitment with an arbitrarily chosen other. And that joy perhaps is the real joy of loving, the joy of reaching out beyond yourself. In caring for the other, you transcend yourself.

SHE: Whether or not the other "turns you on"?

HE: Yeah. Can't you imagine a society where the emphasis is on developing mature or caring persons and once developed, such persons could be randomly paired up to create as best they could a unique and productive relationship?

232

SHE: I don't know.

HE: You don't believe that I am the only male on this planet whom you could love, do you?

SHE: Yes—no—yes. I mean, I don't believe that in one sense, but then again I can't imagine loving anyone else. To suggest that I could love anybody else somehow conveys the idea that what I love in you is a projection of myself; and I can't believe this, I don't feel it.

HE: Lovers can't analyze love.

SHE: Nonlovers can't analyze it, either. (Pause) Look, there's something wrong with what you said before. You said that love which is under the sway of passion is forced, that it is given in hopes of return only. That's not right. My love for you is passionate, and I feel it as a force. I admire you, I respect you, I esteem you. But I don't love you *because* you love me or because you are nice to me. And I don't believe I love you in the hopes of your loving me. I am proud that you love me, I wouldn't want you not to love me; but I don't love you in order to get you to love me.

HE: If I loved you to get you to care for me, I would think I was using you; and I sure wouldn't want to believe that of myself. But is that delusion? Is it self-deceit? What could cause us to fall out of love unless it were that one felt that the other no longer cared? If I began to suspect that you didn't like me, would this make me no longer hold you in high regard? And would this in turn make me no longer love you? And would this prove that I loved

233

you all along only for what you could give me?

SHE: Whoa. We don't understand the falling-out-of-love process well enough to know what it is like. But it doesn't follow that because a couple falls out of love that they were using each other all along.

HE: I've heard people who have fallen out of love say it was all just a physical attraction anyway.

SHE: I've heard them talk about loving but not liking.

HE: I've heard them saying they never were in love.

SHE: Or how about "the spark has gone out of our relationship."

HE: But I can't remember hearing people say how they could have avoided falling out of love.

SHE: Just like we can't account for why we *are* in love. I can't tell why I love you. It is just a reality. It is a brute fact.

HE: It would sound foolish to advise someone how to fall in love.

SHE: Yet people who fall in love have to be prepared for the possibility of falling in love. And I don't think it would be foolish to advise somebody how to love or how to stay in love.

HE: I kind of rely on my feelings to "tell" me what to do. But sometimes I do reflect on what I've done and wonder if it was "right."

SHE: Yet I can't see a technology of love, a science of loving. That would make it seem too much like manipulation again.

HE: Would it make sense to talk of preparation for the possibility of staying in love?

SHE: I am prepared for that possibility and only that possibility.

HE: As I experience it, it is only through a great act of imagination that I can picture us not in love. It is part of the meaning of love that it includes permanence. For if love is a reaching beyond yourself, then it doesn't make sense to think of it in temporary terms.

SHE: In the abstract, I can talk about such possibilities as being self-sufficient, being in love with several persons at one time, or even being in love on a temporary basis; but in the concrete, these possibilities seem remote. I know that what appears solid is really composed of mostly empty space but atoms and molecules and subatomic particles seem as remote to "reality" as these alternatives to love seem to the reality of my relationship to you.

HE: And in the concrete, I experience our love not only as almost solid, but as alive, in the sense that it is incomplete.

SHE: As something growing.

HE: As something changing. It is a striving for an ideal; so I experience it as something that will be even better. As such, I have to be aware that it may ferment as well as flourish. As a striving for an ideal, it is something I feel in common with all other lovers.

SHE: People exposed to other ideals or other values might be striving towards other goals, like an artist is always striving to the perfect art-work or a scientist striving towards truth.

* * *

At this point, it became obvious to all of us that I was eavesdropping, so I turned into a convenient doorway. If these young lovers get to read this, I hope that I got the gist of what they said and I thank them for their contribution to this symposium.

Author Index

Subject Index

240

Subject Index

Subject Index

Objective discussion, 69
Objectivity, 80
Occupational sector, 45, 47
Oedipal, 163, 216
Oppression, 79
Oral, 164
Organism, living, 78
Organs, 70
Orgasm, 83

Panic, (-ed), 152
Paranoia, (-oid), 152, 153
Parents, 70
Partners, marital, 221
Passion, 231
Passivity, 92
Pathological, 84, 102, 105
Pathology, 71
Patient, (s), 143-171
Peers, 70
Person, mature, xiv
Personality, 72, 90
  homosexual, 129
Personal-social repertory, 201
Philosophy, 90
  Judeo-Christian, 91
Phobic, 157
Physical, 74, 77
Physical attraction, 234
Physiological,
  indicies, 73
Pleasure, 79
Poetic license, 69
Poetry, 69
Position, job-occupational, 58
Positivist, 73
Possessions, material, 41, 46
Pregenital, 72
Premature ejaculation, 149
Prestige, 58
Pressures, social, 7, 73
Procedures, scientific, 69
Prose, 69
Psychiatrist, (s), 147, 171
Psychoanalytic, 70
  theory, 6
  views against, 176 ff
Psychological, 77

Psychologists, 102, 104
Psychologizing, 91
Psychotherapy, (-eutic), (-ist), 143,
  144, 146, 148, 149, 152, 154,
  162, 163
Psychotic, 152

Quantitatively, 73

Rational-emotive psychology, 178
Rationalization, (s), 81, 144, 156
Reality, 74, 84
Reason, 80
Regard, unconditional positive,
  192
Regression, (-ive), 159, 164
Reject, (-ed), 156, 163
Relate, 75
Relation, (s), 70, 81
  interpersonal, xiii
Relationship, (s), 147, 150, 153-
  155, 157, 161, 164, 169
  pre-existing, 72
  primary, 63
  psychotherapeutic, 90
  secondary, 63
  temporal, 83
Religion, (-ous), (s), 14-16, 23, 73,
  90
Repression, 71, 79
Respect, xiii, 22, 219, 220, 224,
  226
  for others, xiv, 22
  for self, xiv, 22
  in religion, 226
Response, physiological, 83
Responsibility, 84, 146, 220, 224
Reunion, 71
Revolution, 79
Reward, (s), 86
  -value system, 53 ff
Rights, womens, 26, 98, 104
Risks, 80
Roles,
  husband-father, 45, 46
  wife-mother, 45

S-R bonds, 81

243